First published in the United Kingdom in 2017 by
Pavilion
43 Great Ormond Street
London
WC1N 3HZ

ISBN 978-1-91121-673-5

A CIP catalogue record for this book is available
from the British Library.

10 9 8 7 6 5 4 3 2 1

Reproduction by Mission Productions, Hong Kong
Printed and bound by Toppan Leefung Printing
Ltd, China

This book can be ordered direct from the publisher
at www.pavilionbooks.com

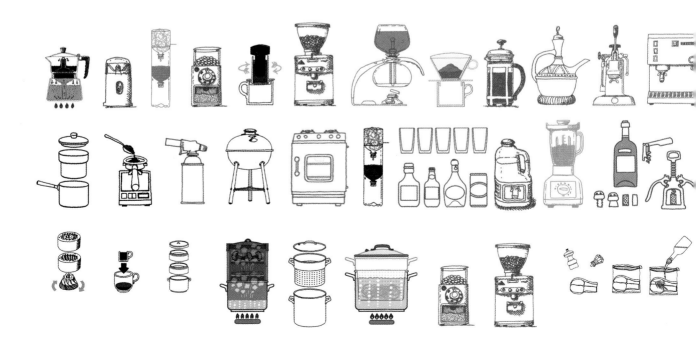

SNOW'S

KITCHENALIA

how everything works

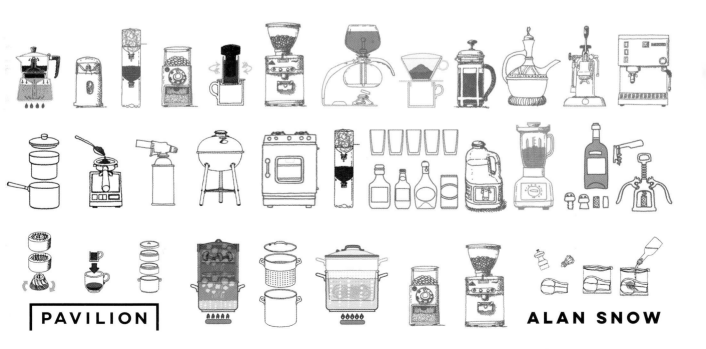

PAVILION

ALAN SNOW

CONTENTS

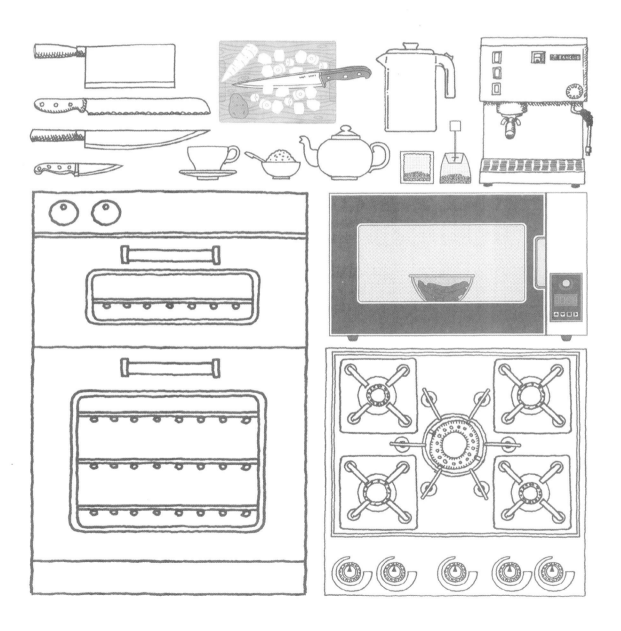

KITCHENALIA

There are many books on food for the home cook, but few which can quickly answer questions about the organization of the kitchen, and the usage of its equipment. The purpose of this book is to act as a useful reference guide by giving background information on the kitchen, the tools found there for food preparation, layout, and storage. I hope it will be a 'go to' book on the kitchen shelf for when questions arise that involve the actual kitchen, and the equipment used with food, while also helping to make cooking more enjoyable, and understandable.

ALAN SNOW

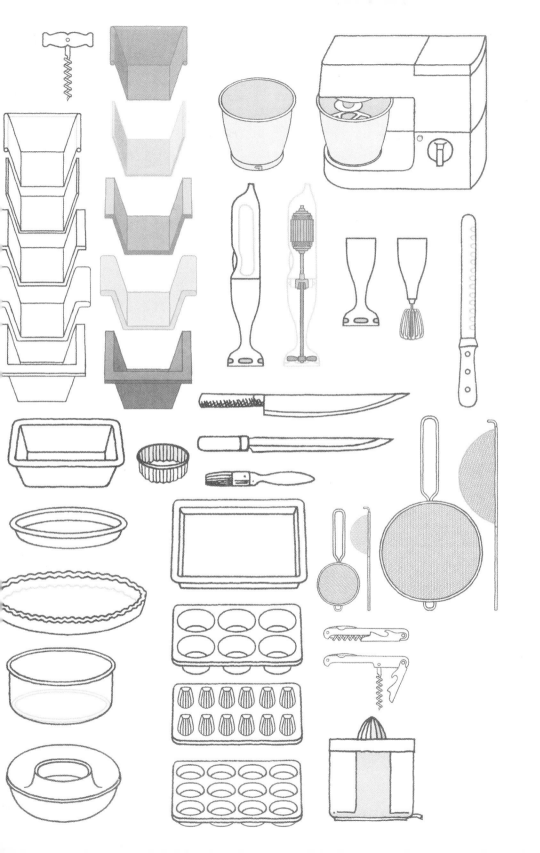

TOOLS

TOOLS

INTRODUCING KITCHEN KNIVES

Kitchen knives in the West have evolved to cover single and multiple functions, and we now find ourselves with a huge choice of not only of Western-style knives but also designs from other parts of the world. It is not necessary to own or use a huge range of knives, and one should bear in mind the adage: 'A sharp, cheap knife is worth more than the most expensive knife blunt.'

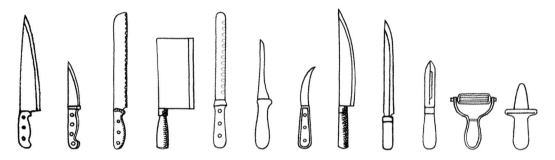

Kitchen knives have developed over more than 1,000 years, but the basic parts remain the same in most of them.

PARTS OF A KNIFE

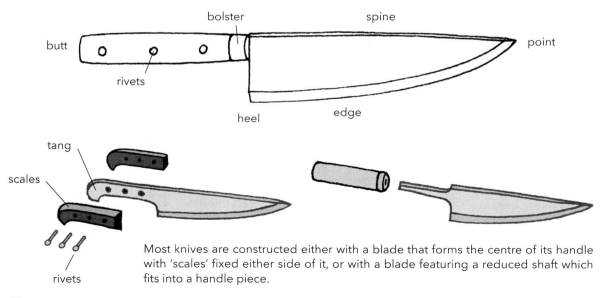

Most knives are constructed either with a blade that forms the centre of its handle with 'scales' fixed either side of it, or with a blade featuring a reduced shaft which fits into a handle piece.

Recently, moulded one-piece knives have become more common and these often have a hollow handle that helps with the balance of the knife.

Metal knives are sharpened by grinding metal away until the edge is really sharp (see pages 20–21). The angle of the blade sides and the angle that the grinder is held at vary a great deal. On Western knives, the edge is usually ground on both sides. By contrast, Japanese knives are traditionally ground away from one side. This produces a knife that moves to one side as it cuts. Though unusual, it is possible to buy left-handed Japanese knives but not in all brands. Serrated bread knives are again sharpened with a bias to one side; it is worth buying a decent one that suits your 'handedness' because it will both make cutting considerably easier and will probably last a lifetime, too.

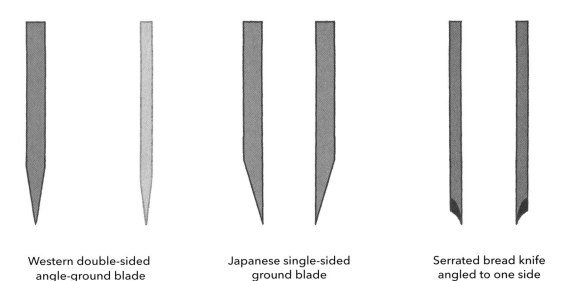

Western double-sided angle-ground blade

Japanese single-sided ground blade

Serrated bread knife angled to one side

TYPES OF KITCHEN KNIVES

CHEF'S KNIFE

blade size 20–25 cm (8–10 inches)

The chef's knife is probably the single most-used knife in Western cookery. It is one of the 'three essential knives'. Its shape varies regionally, but the basic shape is very similar to a symmetrically sharpened Japanese Santonku chef's knife (see right). It can be used for most jobs but a smaller or more flexible blade may have advantages in some cases.

PARING KNIFE

blade size 7.5–10 cm (3–4 inches)

The paring knife is the second essential kitchen knife, and it handles almost anything that requires delicacy, or anything that is too small for the chef's knife. Again, similar knives are used in kitchens across the world. The paring knife can be used for trimming, peeling, and slicing smaller fruits and vegetables.

BREAD KNIFE

blade size 20–30 cm (8–12 inches)

In any household where bread is a feature, a bread knife is the third essential knife. The serrated blade avoids tearing the bread. It can also be used on softer fruit and vegetables (such as tomatoes) with good results. If you are left-handed, do try to find a left-handed bread knife, because it will make a vast difference to how well it performs.

FILLETING KNIFE

blade size 12.5–18 cm (5–7 inches)

The filleting knife is finely shaped to allow manoeuvring while cutting. Similar but slimmer than a boning knife (see right), it is also very flexible, which makes it especially suitable for working with fish. However, unless you are a very keen cook, it is not absolutely essential.

CARVING KNIFE

blade size 23–30 cm (9–12 inches)

The carving knife is one of the longest knives in the kitchen. It is shaped this way to cut meat with a continuous movement so as to avoid tearing it. They are usually quite flexible so as to allow them to move around bones. This function can be covered to some extent by a sharp chef's knife if you do not have a carving knife.

PEELING KNIFE

blade size 6.5–9 cm (2½–3½ inches)

The peeling knife is used to remove skins from fruit and vegetables. It is used by drawing the curved blade towards you through the fruit or vegetable. It works far better than a paring knife because the blade is designed to work with the curve of whatever you are peeling. In most cases, you will find a simple peeler (see right) more convenient, though.

BONING KNIFE

blade size 12.5-18 cm (5-7 inches)

The boning knife fulfils the function or removing bones and dividing joints and cuts of meat. This knife is necessary if you intend to butcher your own meat and want a tidy result. Butchery takes knowledge, practice and skill that can take years to perfect, but if you use a very sharp boning knife and work slowly and carefully, you can achieve good results.

JAPANESE SANTOKU

blade size 20-25 cm (8-10 inches)

This is the general-purpose chef's knife in the Japan. It is used as a cleaver as well as a cutting blade. One side of the blade is sharpened (so the blade is not symmetrical), and so it has to be used in slightly different way to cut. They are also available with a symmetrically sharpened blade, though, for the Western market.

YANAGIBI

blade size 25-30 cm (10-12 inches)

This is the knife used for cutting sushi and sashimi. The length of the knife allows it to be drawn through the fish to make a single cut in one complete movement. It is more akin to the Western carving knives than a Western filleting knife. Like the Japanese Santoku, it is sharpened to one side.

SERRATED VEGETABLE KNIFE

blade size 8-12 cm (3-5 inches)

Small serrated vegetable knives are extremely useful. If you buy one of the professional branded ones, they are often the cheapest item in their range, but very sharp and can be used for many jobs (not just vegetables). They are difficult to sharpen, though, so add a new one to your collection if the first one gets blunt and use the old knife for other jobs.

CLEAVER

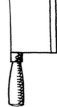

blade size 15-20 cm (6-8 inches)

The cleaver is traditionally used in the West for chopping through bones and for rough butchery, but in large parts of Asia it is the principal chef's tool and replaces the knife for many jobs. In Chinese cookery, meat is nearly always pre-cut using a 'Shun' (similar to the Western cleaver but much more versatile) to aid the speed of cooking.

VEGETABLE PEELER

blade size 5 cm (2 inches) approx.

Vegetable peelers come in various designs but the easier and cheapest to use are the commercial 'two way swing blade' type. They will be serviceable for a good while but are hard to sharpen so once they become blunt replace them.

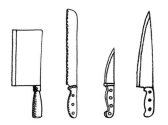
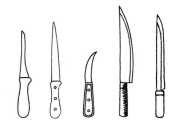

CHOOSING KNIVES

Choosing a new knife is something that should be considered carefully because it is one of the only tools you will probably use every day. There are knives available for almost any price point you can think of – from the cheapest found in supermarkets to custom imported handmade Japanese knives. A lot of professionals use 'industrial quality' rather than artisan-made knives, and these industrial knives are often reasonably priced and very good quality. If you don't use the kitchen a great deal or cannot or don't want to sharpen your knives, then consider very hard bladed knives that will hold an edge for a long time. Ceramic knives come pre-sharpened, and most people don't expect to sharpen them ever. The only downside to them is that they are brittle so they can break if dropped.

WHICH KNIVES?

A chef's knife is a good place to begin because it is versatile and can cut large items as well as small ones. It can cut bread but it's not that easy unless it's extremely sharp, so a bread knife should be considered as a second purchase alongside a small paring knife. The small commercial serrated knives are extremely useful and I would consider this next, alongside a vegetable peeler.

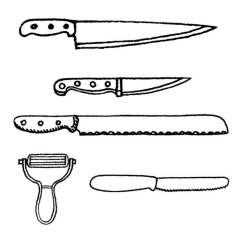

CHEF'S KNIVES

A chef's knife has a number of factors that will affect your choice. The first is the 'fit'. The drop between the heel of the knife and the handle should be enough for you to be able to chop without you banging your knuckles.

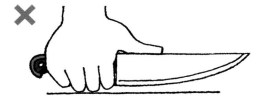
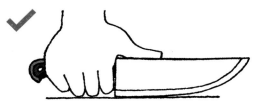

Checking the type of steel a knife is made from will give an indication as to how hard the blade is, how well it will hold an edge, and how much flex the blade possesses. Softer steel means a more heavily flexing blade, which will not hold an edge as well.

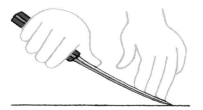 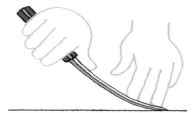

The balance of a knife in your hand is important and will affect your long-term comfort when using the knife. Try holding the knife in a pinch grip on the blade close to the handle to give a good indication of balance, and then try holding the knife for chopping in a hold with your thumb on the back of the handle.

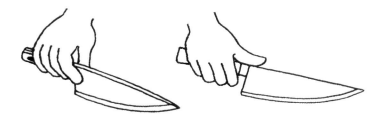

PARING KNIVES

When choosing a paring knife, check the type of steel used and how comfortable the knife is to hold. Though it can be used for slicing and cutting, for peeling and paring, hold the knife in your hand with the blade facing the thumb. The knife should feel comfortable in this position.

BREAD KNIVES

Bread knives should be comfortable in the hand, not too flexible, and as the blade is ground at a single angle to one side you should buy a knife that is left- or right-handed to suit you.

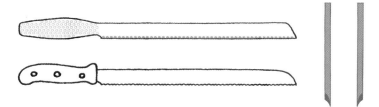

17

USING KNIVES

Professional chefs will spend many hours using knives and many have had specific training to use them. Some chefs practice on vegetables. The home cook can develop reasonable knife skills with practice but there are some basic approaches that should be adhered to.

THE CHEF'S KNIFE

Don't hold the knife with your finger running along the spine of the knife, or grip it like a hammer. Both of these holds will make it more difficult to control the blade.

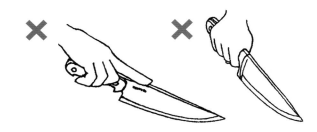

SLICING

For slicing, hold the knife in a relaxed pinch grip. The blade should be sharp so that drawing it through the food will be enough to do the cutting, with no 'sawing'.

CHOPPING

For chopping, hold the knife with your thumb next to the back of the blade and bring the knife up and down in a rocking motion. When finely chopping things, add pressure with the other hand on the back of the blade.

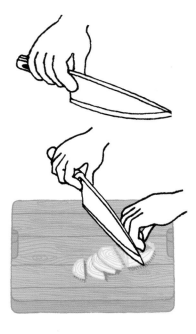

CARVING

Allow the meat to 'rest' after taking it out from the oven, then place it on a board (or on a large plate so you can cut low into the meat without catching the edge of the plate). Use a fork to hold the meat still as you draw the knife through the meat in a smooth continuous motion, across the grain. Going across the grain produces a more tender mouthful.

CHOPPING BOARDS

In commercial kitchens as many as six different chopping boards are used to maintain food hygiene, and to avoid flavours contaminating each other.

red = raw meat	blue = fish	yellow = cooked meats	green = mild flavoured fruit and veg	brown = strong-flavoured fruit and veg	white = dairy

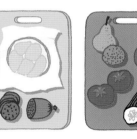

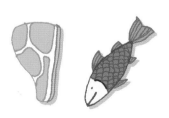

This is excessive for the smaller-scale home kitchen, but it's sensible to use at least two chopping boards – one for raw fish and meat, and another for cooked food, dairy, and fruit and vegetables. Plastic may be better for the meat and fish board and the other can be wood. If you use the wooden board for strong-flavoured vegetables or herbs (like garlic), you can reserve one side for them to avoid flavour transfer.

19

 # SHARPENING KNIVES

Knife sharpeners vary in quality a lot, and cheap versions may produce a sharp edge but it may not be even, and may take off a lot of metal and reduce the life of the knife. Good modern sharpeners are more than adequate if you're careful about how you use them. Most knives are sharpened at an angle close to 22 degrees, and while you may want to deviate from this, it is wise to try to maintain the same angle along the length of the blade. This can be learnt with practice, but there are a couple of ways to help with this when using a stone to sharpen the knife: you can draw a line down the edge of the blade with a marker pen or use a device that holds the knife at the correct angle as you work. If you are buying knives and a sharpening steel, note that the steel has to be made of a harder metal than the knives.

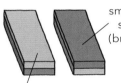

smooth side (brown)

rough side (grey)

USING A SHARPENING STONE

Using a sharpening stone as a sharpening tool will be necessary at some point in a knife's life unless you constantly maintain it with a sharpening steel or other device. Sharpening stones usually feature two different grades of abrasion (one on each side) and usually need to be lubricated with oil or water. Note that if you ever use oil on a stone you will have to carry on using oil as it will stop water from soaking into the stone. If you choose to use water, then soak the stone for 30 minutes before you use it, then place it on a surface where it won't slide/move. If you use oil, you can apply a few drops when you are about to start.

Unless your knife is already sharp and you're just refining it, start with the rough side of the stone. Hold the handle in one hand and apply gentle pressure with the fingers of the other hand as you draw the knife along and across the stone, from handle to knife tip. Some draw the knife towards themselves as the blade is facing away from them; others push the blade away. Find the method that you feel has the best control over the angle of the blade as you work. Before you start, inspect the knife for any dents or notches. The sharpening should grind away enough of the edge to remove this damage. This should be done on the rough side of the stone. Once this is done and any rounding off of the blade is corrected, you can turn over the knife and refine the sharpening with the smoother surface of the stone.

either move the blade towards you or away from you

22° angle

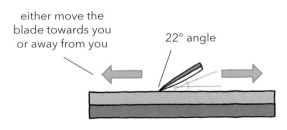

USING A SHARPENING WHEEL

A sharpening wheel typically features two stone wheels (one rough and one smooth) and a water trough that the wheels dip into. To use it, fill the water reservoir, and draw the knife through the slot with the rough or smooth wheel as needed. If you use one of these sharpeners regularly you may only need to use the 'fine' (smooth) wheel to maintain a very sharp edge.

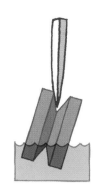

USING A SHARPENING STEEL

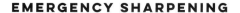

Sharpening steels 'revive' the edge of the blade by bending back any edge that has folded over, and also by adding micro serration to the edge. To use one, hold the blade at the same angle the knife was sharpened at and draw the blade across the steel, then repeat with the blade's other side applied to the other side of the steel. It is not necessary to apply much pressure.

EMERGENCY SHARPENING

If you find yourself in a situation with blunt knives and no sharpening tools, you can use the base of a ceramic bowl as a sharpening stone. Place the bowl upside-down and wet the unglazed bottom edge. Then sharpen as you would with a stone.

22° angle

SPECIALIST KNIVES

There are many specialist knives available for specific purposes in the kitchen and some are more useful than others.

OYSTER KNIVES

Oyster knives are very useful if you want to serve oysters – it's quite difficult to open them safely with other knives. Even with an oyster knife it is still tricky, and if the knife slips it can cause injury, so be very careful. Some chefs wear a chainmail glove to protect their hands.

SHUCKING AN OYSTER

 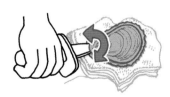 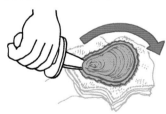

To open an oyster you need to cut the hinge at the wider end of the shell (A), then separate the top shell (B) from the bottom shell and cut the last fixing in the base of the shell (C).

  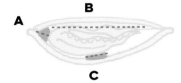

[1] Hold the oyster in a cloth in one hand, and with the other hand, insert the knife tip into the hinge.

[2] Tilt and twist the knife gently to cut and break the hinge.

[3] Draw the knife along the seam of the shell to loosen the lid.

 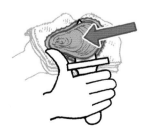 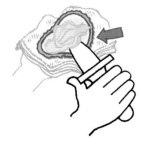

[4] Keep loosening the lid, drawing the knife all the way around.

[5] Cut the oyster from the lid, then lift off the top.

[6] Insert the knife under the flesh of the oyster and cut the last fixing.

MEZZALUNA KNIVES

Single and double-bladed mezzaluna knives are used for cutting herbs very finely, and the single-bladed type can also be used for cutting pizza. Specific chopping boards with a slightly bowled surface are often used to avoid spreading strong herb flavours to other foods.

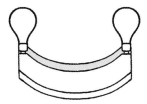

VEGETABLE PEELERS

Vegetable peelers are an essential tool in the kitchen. Though there are various types, the type that chefs prefer is the small, cheap 'speed peeler'; these become blunt over time and are difficult to sharpen, so it's better to buy a new one.

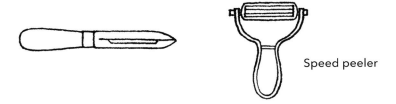

Speed peeler

CHEESE KNIVES, PLANES & GRATERS

Soft sticky cheese can be cut and spread with a butter-type knife, or with a knife with hole in the blade so there is little to stick onto. Medium-soft and hard cheese can be cut with a paring knife, or a serrated knife. Hard and very hard cheese can be shaved with a cheese plane for quite fine slices, or grated using a grater or microplane.

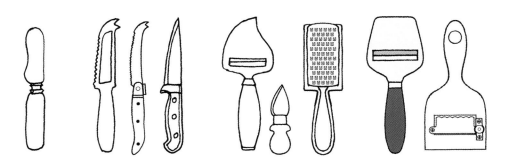

SPOONS, LADLES, SPATULAS & WHISKS

Early spoons were made from ivory, flint, or wood. Wooden spoons are still common in the kitchen and are good heat insulators but can be difficult to sanitize. This is why certain woods with antiseptic qualities have been favoured. Metal is easily sanitized but can become too hot to hold unless it features an insulated handle. Silicone tools are a good option because they can be easily sanitized, and act as an insulator.

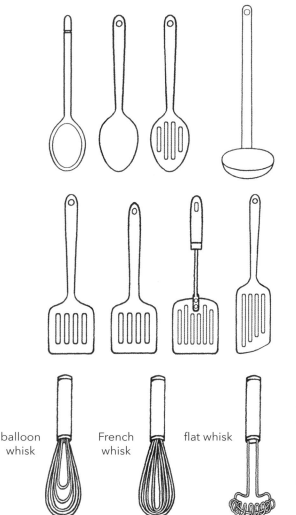

Spoons are inexpensive and a selection of different types is very useful for both cooking and serving. These should include, a large spoon, a slotted spoon, and a ladle.

Spatulas are very useful for pan-frying and turning when grilling. They are usually made from metal, plastic, or silicone. However, be careful to avoid using metal ones with non-stick surfaces.

balloon whisk

French whisk

flat whisk

Hand whisks are useful when only light whipping is required and there are different types for various jobs. Balloon whisks and French whisks look very similar, but the balloon whisk is lighter and used for whisking eggs, etc., while the French whisk is used for heavier sauces. Flat or spring whisks are good for making sauces in pans as they can get into corners.

SIEVES

Fine sieves are an essential tool for all but the most basic of cooking. From sifting flour, to de-seeding soft stewed fruit, or removing lumps from sauces, all of these can be done easily with a sieve. The common rounded sieve can be used with a large spoon or soft spatula to help pass food through them such as sauces. A small rounded sieve can also be used for straining liquids while pouring them, such as with tea. Avoid plastic sieves if you are straining anything hot.

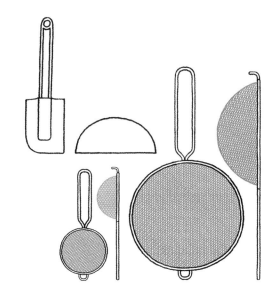

COLANDERS

Colanders are very useful for everything from draining hot boiled potatoes safely to rinsing salad. A metal colander that can withstand boiling water is preferable to a plastic one that can only be used with cold foods. Very coarse plastic sieves are good for holding vegetables that you are going to wash in the sink.

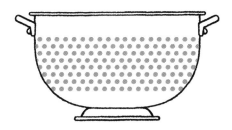

CHINOISE SIEVES

Chinoise sieves are common in commercial kitchens and are more useful than a simple rounded sieve for many jobs. As they come with different sizes of mesh, you can use them to remove particles of different sizes. You can place a coarse Chinoise sieve inside a fine sieve and sift a mixture in two stages, if needed.

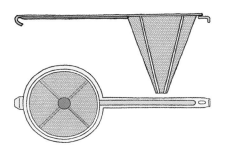
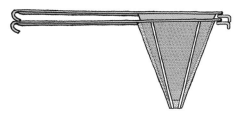

GRATERS, SLICERS & PEELERS

There are many types of grater but the basic multisided graters will cover most jobs in the kitchen. Buy a good one that doesn't flex when you lean on it and is large enough to get a cleaning brush inside.

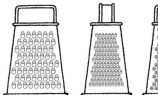

NUTMEG GRATER

If you like nutmeg, then a nutmeg grater will come in very handy because freshly ground nutmeg is vastly superior to the pre-bought alternative. Many models feature a compartment for storing the nutmeg between uses.

GRATERS WITH STORAGE

Graters with self-contained storage in the form a of catch container do work but grated food often degrades quickly so it's better not to store anything longer than necessary.

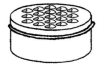

MICROPLANE

Microplanes were originally used for woodworking but they now feature in many kitchens. The fineness of the texture they can produce means that they are especially handy for grating foods like chocolate, coconut, and ginger.

ROTARY GRATER

Rotary graters are turned via a handle and are commonly used for grating hard cheeses (such as Parmesan), but they are also extremely good for grating nuts.

MANDOLINE SLICER

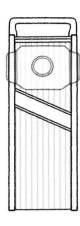

Metal mandoline slicers were at one time restricted to professional kitchen, as they were expensive but plastic versions are available quite cheaply. They are **dangerous**, though, and should be kept away from children. But if operated correctly and used with great care, you can produce some very finely sliced foods. They are particularly useful in the preparation of salads, for cutting potatoes into chips or fries or preparing vegetables to be deep fried. Read the instructions, be careful and do it at your own risk…

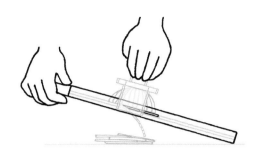

SPIRAL VEGETABLE SHREDDERS

These have become more common recently, because it makes it easy to prepare vegetables in the form of shredded salads and for pasta and noodle replacements. Many vegetables have a much lower calorific value than the wheat flour commonly used in noodles so some may find that investing in one of these is a particularly good idea. Please be aware that they can be extremely sharp.

CORERS & PEELERS

There are a number of devices for coring and peeling. Corers are particularly useful for coring fruit if you wish to bake it stuffed but in a single piece, as with baked apples. It avoids slightly dangerous knife work when trying to get the centre of the fruit out. Segmenters that you can push down on fruit to remove the core and divide the rest of the fruit into smaller sections can be useful when preparing fruit for cooked dishes or for small children. Rotary peelers are now available very cheaply. These are similar to a device developed in the Victorian period, and there is a certain wondrousness about seeing them work today. Although it can be as quick to use a knife or speed peeler, children love them.

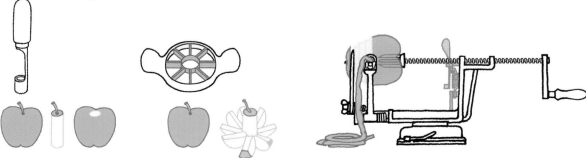

SCALES

Systems for weighing objects have been in use for 6,000 years, and the root of this probably lies in early trading. Some cultures have used weights in the kitchen for measurement, while others have used volume. The USA still uses the 'cup' system for measuring dry goods, while in Europe, the metric system (kilograms and grams) is used, while volume for liquids is measured in millilitres and litres. In Europe, there is also the standard reference to teaspoons and tablespoons for smaller quantities. In the professional kitchen, some volume measures are used, but increasingly things are weighed using the metric system.

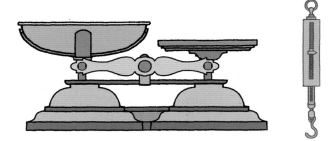 

Before digital scales, two different types of scale were commonly used: balance scales, which involved placing items of equal mass onto two platforms or pans, and spring scales, which records the distance that a spring moves under a load.

Digital scales make life easier than with balance or spring scales because they have a 'Tare' function. This is to 'zero' the scales after you have placed a container on them so you can measure just the weight of the food or liquid. Nearly all digital scales feature both metric and Imperial measures. If you do a lot of baking or wish to record measurements for spices or other flavourings which are small in quality, then consider buying a second set of smaller scales that can measure to fractions of a gram, because large scales rarely function well measuring small quantities.

VOLUME MEASURES

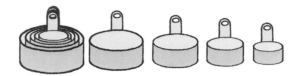

A 'pinch' or a 'handful' must have been the first measurements used in cooking, and containers and implements like spoons became measures as soon as they were used. Standardized measures would have become regional and then wider as trading spread. There are still many local variations of measurements across the world. As stated earlier, it is often far easier to measure by weight for all ingredients if you wish to get consistent results (particularly with dry foods). The weight of volumes of any particular food will vary if the food has 'settled', or if it is of a slightly different texture, and/or if the containers are not equally filled. This is particularly important with baking where the results can be affected badly by minor variations. Unless you use American recipes from books or the Internet, the advice is generally to avoid the American cup system, or if you find a recipe that you like, convert it to weights and note them down.

VOLUME MEASURING LIQUIDS

Liquids are relatively easy to measure by volume and a measuring jug (pitcher) will usually be adequate. For finer measurements, cone-shaped measuring beakers work well as the measure becomes more precise as the quantity of liquid becomes smaller. If you're after something even more precise (usually for baking), a large plastic syringe can be very useful. Basters with measures along the outside are also very convenient for drawing off an exact amount of liquid.

NOTE: Liquids do vary in density

1 litre water = 1,000 grams
1 litre olive oil = 912 grams
1 litre corn/golden syrup = 1,441 grams
1 litre vodka = 947 grams
1 litre ethanol = 789 grams

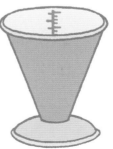

BAKEWARE

Bakeware is available in many materials, each with a number of different attributes that make them suitable for baking.

Tinned steel is a traditional material for baking. It works well and is reasonably cheap, but the tinned surface can wear. To avoid rusting, you should hand-wash it, avoid scrubbing, then dry immediately.

Aluminium is light, transmits heat very well, releases baked goods from the tin readily, and is easily cleaned. Many professionals prefer aluminium.

Non-stick bakeware is great as long as you avoid damaging the coating. For light cakes such as sponges, try to avoid heavy tins that do not transmit heat quickly.

Glass and **ceramic** are very slow to transmit heat, but for very long cook times for recipes such as pies, they work very well. Avoid for cake baking.

Silicone bakeware is good for its release properties and ease of cleaning, but for large cakes there is risk of spillage from the flex in the mould. Use a baking tray to support larger moulds if there is a risk of spillage, while carrying the cake to the oven, or while baking.

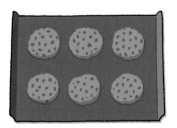

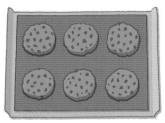

RELEASE AFTER BAKING

There are a number of ways to help release baked goods after baking. On plain metal such as tinned steel, you can use grease or light oil. With non-stick surfaces, it depends on the recipe, but if you have any problems, try greasing very lightly. For some types of baking such as biscuits (cookies), you can use greaseproof paper as this will flex and allow you to remove it from the baked items once cooled. There are now flat silicone sheets for baking on and these are very good.

BAKEWARE CONTAINERS

Not only is bakeware available in many materials, but also a in huge range of shapes. These range from moulds for funeral biscuits from Japan to Scandinavian ring cake tins. A few standard moulds will cover most baking recipes.

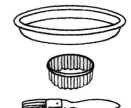

Sponge tins are used to bake shallow cakes for layering. They can also be used for flans and shallow pies. It's worth buying at least two if you intend to bake cakes.

Standard cake tins are used to cook deep cakes, but these cakes can also be sliced horizontally when cool to make a layered cake. Many have a base that is removable and can be used to lift the cake out once cooked.

Springform cake tins have a loosening latch on one side so they can open and separate from the cooked cake. These are used by many professionals.

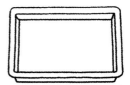

Ring moulds are used primarily for Bundt-style cakes, but they can also be used for pies or terrines. The ring shape's lack of depth allows the cake to cook faster and more evenly.

Swiss roll tins are flat tins with a raised lip, which creates a very shallow cake. Once cooked, it can be coated with a filling and rolled to form a finished rolled cake. These tins are extremely useful for lots of other cooking jobs, including roasting, baking biscuits (cookies), drying, and for fridge cakes.

Muffin tins are for baking… muffins but can be used for individual pies, etc. As with cupcake moulds and moulds for Madeleines or other small shaped cakes, the tin is usually greased (if they aren't non-stick or silicone), and sometimes floured before the mixture is added.

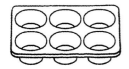
Six-hole muffin tin

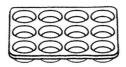
12-hole mini muffin tin

Madeleine tin

FOOD MIXERS

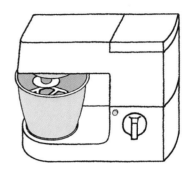

Hobart Corporation is credited with the invention of the modern electric 'stand' food mixer in 1914 in Ohio, USA. The first machines were large and were used commercially; they were also installed in ships by the US Navy. In 1917, smaller domestic versions were introduced under the name KitchenAid. They became popular during the 1920s and the Model 'K' – the basis of the modern KitchenAid mixer design – was developed in the 1930s. During the 1930s, an engineer at the rival Sunbeam company developed the first dual-whisk mixer, launched as the Mixmaster. This became the most popular mixer in the 1950s and 1960s, but by the mid-1990s, the company declined, and KitchenAid became the main brand of mixer in large parts of the world. In the UK, the Kenwood mixer was developed in the early 1950s and dominated the market until KitchenAid mixers became popular in the 1990s. There are now many mixers on the market, but most emulate these two original designs.

ATTACHMENTS

There is a huge choice of attachments, and while some work well, others are gimmicks. Alternative mixing attachments to fix in the main drive such as whisks and dough hooks are well worth using, as are mincers and blenders. If you are interested in other attachments, do some research: e.g. some pasta extruding attachments don't work well because real pasta machines need extremely powerful motors to push the dough through.

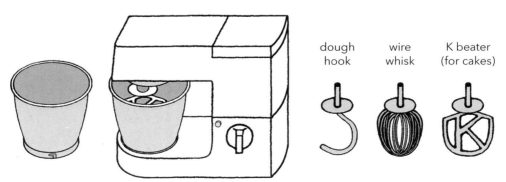

dough hook · wire whisk · K beater (for cakes)

FOOD PROCESSORS

Food processors have much in common with stand mixers but are usually driven from below rather than above. This makes them more like blenders but with a wider base and more attachments. The term 'food processor' was originally not limited to electrically driven devices but included hand-powered machines. The first electric food processor was designed in Germany in 1947 and was little more than a blender with a lot of attachments, but in 1960 the French company Robot Coupe started selling an industrial-quality food processor to the catering trade. They are still popular across the world today. In 1972, Robot Coupe introduced a domestic machine called 'the Magimix', and this quickly became popular. In 1973, Magimix was imported to the US, modified and sold by Carl Sontheimer under the brand name Cuisinart. Sontheimer carried on with improvements for another 15 years until he sold the company.

Food processors were originally designed for shredding and slicing, but have attachments for mixing, and even whisking. They are generally smaller and less expensive than stand mixers, so if your cooking does not involve a large amount of baking then it may be a good option. If you want to do a lot of baking, then a stand mixer is a better choice.

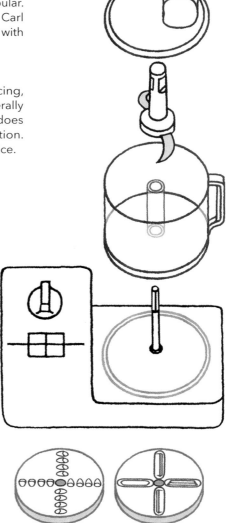

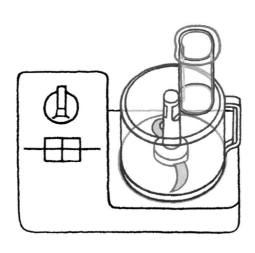

HAND MIXERS & WHISKS

HAND WHISKS

Hand-operated mechanical whisks were invented in the 19th century and were very much the gadget of the day, with hundreds of variations produced by different suppliers. They are still available, and they are a fairly cheap option if you only have limited need for a whisk. However, a balloon whisk can give you as good, if not better results.

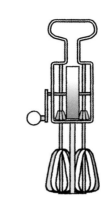

HAND ELECTRIC MIXER/WHISKS

The Sunbeam company introduced the electric twin whisk on their Mixmaster models, but these mixers had other attachments for mixing and even for dough. The mixer also could be detached from the stand and used as a hand mixer. Electric hand mixers take up considerably less space than either a food processor or a stand mixer, they are much cheaper, and they perform at least a good proportion of the tasks the larger machines do. They are useful but probably not the tool for a serious baker.

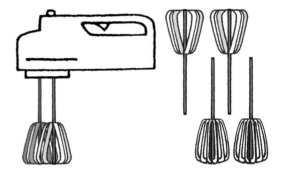

STICK BLENDERS

Stick blenders usually come with two attachments – the blender and a whisk. The blender is particularly useful when it is necessary to blend something hot, because the blender can be placed in the pan rather than having to empty the pan into a blender container. They are very good at producing smooth sauces, custards, and soups, but not very good at blending anything featuring large pieces. You will frequently find them in commercial kitchens where they get a lot of use. Some blenders cover a wide number of attachments but these are often limited in size.

As a rule, place the end of the blender stick well below the surface of whatever you want to blend to avoid spattering. The whisks are also useful for beating batters and egg whites.

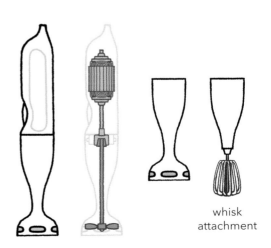

whisk
attachment

THERMOMETERS

oven-suitable shelf
thermometer

heat-probe thermometer

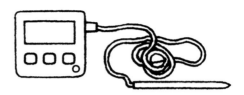

digital meat thermometer

hand-held laser thermometer

sugar
thermometer

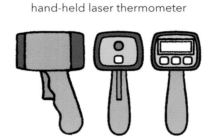

Thermometers are extremely useful and are probably the cheapest upgrade that will make a huge difference in a kitchen.

An oven-suitable shelf thermometer is a useful addition as it will give you a much better reading of the oven's temperature, and of variations in temperature across different parts of the oven.

The process of cooking changes the chemical structure of food, and these changes happen at certain temperatures. Bacteria is also affected by heat and you can judge when you have reduced or killed off any bacteria by measuring the food's temperature. To measure a food's temperature you need to be able to measure it internally, because thickness and fat, sugar, or water content will mean that food heats up at different rates. To do this, use a heat-probe thermometer that you can insert into the food to test it. While you can use a hand-held probe, you can also buy probes that can be inserted into the food and set off an alarm when a desired heat is reached as well as displaying the temperature on a unit outside of the oven.

Sugar thermometers are used to measure the temperature of a sugar solution (such as a jam or syrup), and as the temperature rises and the water content reduces, the thermometer acts as a guide to the consistency of the final cooled product. In the upper range of temperatures, it will measure when the sugar starts to caramelize and brown.

Hand-held laser thermometers are now becoming affordable and can be useful for measuring the heat of sugar solutions, oven temperature, or anything else that doesn't need to be checked internally. They also greatly amuse children.

FOOD GRINDERS & MILLS

PESTLE & MORTAR

The pestle and mortar is used across the planet. In Western kitchens, quite smooth surfaces are common on both the pestle and the mortar, whereas they tend to be of a rougher consistency in the East. The latter can be more useful as modern Western pestle and mortars are often based on those used in pharmacies for grinding fine powders rather than foods.

PEPPER GRINDER

The modern pepper grinder is based on the design by the Peugeot family (who also designed coffee grinders and bicycles before becoming a car manufacturer). Their modern grinders are still regarded as one of the best. Before them a pestle and mortar was used. Pepper loses its freshness quite shortly after grinding, so it's sensible to grind as needed.

MEXICAN METATE

The Mexican metate is the traditional grinding tool base that has been used in South and Central America for over 1,000 years, but similar grinders are found in many parts of the world, including India. It comprises a grinding stone which is moved back and forth over a flat or bowled surface. It was originally used for grinding corn and chocolate, but modern versions can be used to grind a wide range of foods. However, they are large, heavy, and tiring to use on large amount of food.

BLADE GRINDERS

Blade grinders are cheap and useful in the kitchen for purposes other than just coffee. They can be used to grind herbs, hard spices, etc. Some are waterproof so they can be used as a small blender. If you drink a lot of coffee, I would advise buying a second grinder so you don't taint the taste of the coffee.

OIL MILLS

Hand-powered oil mills are useful for making really high-quality oils at home. Piteba of Holland make one that can be used at home and can extract as much as 70% of the oil from grains and nuts. This takes time and effort but the quality of the oil is extremely high.

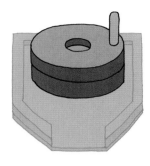

GRAIN MILLS

Grain mills have been used for thousands of years and designs similar to very early ones are still available and used. In Japan, small stone mills are used to grind grains for noodles in some homes and restaurants, and these mills can be purchased online.

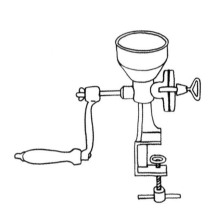

Hand mill

Electric mill

Metal hand grain mills are also available to purchase, but take quite a lot of effort to use. In Northern Europe, there are a number of electric stone grinding mills designed for use at home and if you like wholemeal (wholewheat) flour, they are easy and convenient. Instead of measuring out flour, you simply measure the same weight in grain and tip it into the mill and wait for a minute or so for it to grind the flour. These mills have settings for flour grain size so you can choose how coarse a flour you want. There is some noticeable difference in the flavour of freshly milled flour, and in some studies it was noted that there was a rapid drop off of nutritional value of the flour after only 48 hours after grinding.

WET GRINDERS

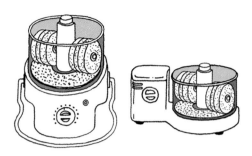

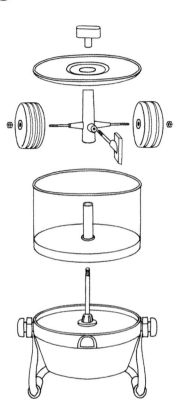

Wet grinders originated in southern India but they are starting to become more common in the West. They are used to grind dhal from beans, lentils, or rice, produce batters for making dosa, and often come with a dough hook so they can be used to make dough for other styles of bread. As they are similar in function to chocolate processing grinders, it is possible to make chocolate from nib through to final processed chocolate, which is ready to mould. The other thing they are very good at is making nut butters.

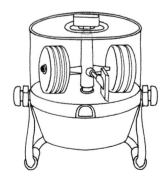

Wet grinders feature a base with a strong motor, a bowl with a base made of granite, two grinding wheels (also made of granite), a central column which holds a scraper and the wheels as they rotate against the bowl base, and a lid and a screw to hold the column in place. These machines are robustly built and reliable, but shouldn't be expected to break down very hard, large particles, so it is best to blend larger foods before adding them to the mill.

MAKING CHOCOLATE

Making chocolate from cacao nibs is surprisingly easy with a wet grinder. Recipes are widely available online, but in order to make solid, well-tempered chocolate, you should aim for the finished chocolate to be between 41–45% fat, which includes dairy fats if you use a milk powder that contains them.

To ease the load on the grinder, place the nibs in a blender. You can do this on their own or add melted cocoa butter (after melting it in a microwave or bain-marie). Blend a little at a time, then add it slowly to the grinder while it's running. Most wet grinders will work best with a load of 1–2 kg (2 lb 3 oz–4 lb 7 oz). Once the nibs are starting to become smooth (perhaps 1 hour in), start to add the rest of the cocoa butter and vanilla pods/beans (if you're using vanilla extract add it later in the process as it will not have to be ground).

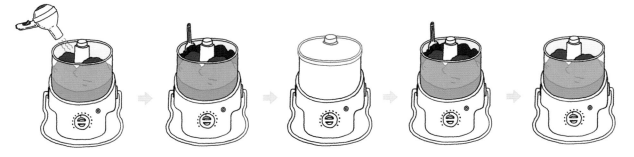

The mix may collect around the stones and column if the temperature is cool. If so, use a hairdryer to warm the mix; once the grinder is running well, it will generate enough heat to kept the mix warm. Check occasionally and scape down any build-up into the mix. After 18 hours the chocolate will start to be worth using, but the particle size will not be that fine. You can continue to run the machine for another 36 hours if you wish. Take samples and allow to cool before tasting. When you are happy, tip the chocolate into a container to cool. It is then ready to temper and mould. Some people add lecthin now to aid tempering.

OTHER COOKING DEVICES

RICE COOKERS

TOASTERS

Rice cookers are very convenient and reliable for producing well-cooked rice. Originating from Japan, they not only cook rice in their preferred 'sticky' style but also are good for Indian-style rice too (but do check the machine you have). First, measure the rice into the base and add water, then select the desired program on the controls and the rice will start cooking. These machines also have a setting for keeping the rice warm.

People do use these devices to cook other things, including bread, cakes, beans, and vegetables. It is even possible to produce black (caramelized) garlic by using the 'keep warm' setting for extended periods of time (about 9 days), but it is a process that generates a strong smell and may permanently impregnate your rice cooker with the smell of garlic.

Electric toasters were invented in Scotland in 1893, and initially only toasted one side of the bread at a time. The bread was turned manually until an American company added an automatic bread turner, but this was soon replaced by the use of heating elements on both sides of the bread. In 1919, a device was invented that would 'pop up' the bread once it was toasted.

Some toasters now feature wide slots that can accommodate a mesh holder clasping together sandwich, and you can find toasters that come complete with racks for heating croissants and other items above the actual toaster.

It is extremely unwise to use any metal object to retrieve a broken or stuck piece of toast from the machine while it is connected to power. Buy silicone or wooden tongs for the purpose instead, but bear in mind that it is still possible to damage the elements if you're not careful.

PORTABLE ELECTRIC GRILLS

WAFFLE MAKERS

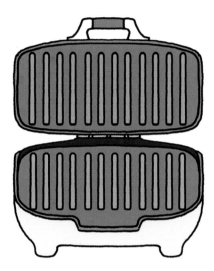

The 'George Foreman Grill' was invented in 1994 by Michael Boehm. The idea was to produce a portable grill to use indoors that would allow fat to drain from the food while cooking (it is sold with a collecting container). With the use of George Foreman as a promotional tool, it became very popular and has since sold over 100 million units. It has also been claimed that it provides a cheap and portable cooking method for the poor, as all that is need is access to an electrical outlet.

It can be used to grill meat, vegetables (it has heating elements both in the base and fold-down lid so cooks evenly), as well as grilled sandwiches. As the grill is tilted, liquids drain off, so it is difficult to cook things such as eggs unless the front is lifted to level the cooking area.

It has been much copied but no one has approached the numbers that the original grill and its variations have sold.

Waffle makers are similar in construction to the portable electric grill but are smaller and have shaped plates that create the familiar shape of a waffle. Some of these machines have changeable plates so the machine can be used for a wider variety of uses, which include grilling sandwiches, making waffle cones for ice cream, potato waffles, scrambled and pressed eggs, and even doughs to make flattened breads.

FRYERS

In the home kitchen, deep-frying can be dangerous and produce lingering smells (few home kitchens have heavy-duty ventilation systems), but with care these problems can be overcome and allow you to produce foods that cannot be replicated in any other way. While it is perfectly possible to deep-fry using a large, deep pan, it is very easy to start a pan fire this way, so it is perhaps safer to use a device such as an electric open fryer or an electric deep-frying machine.

Whichever route you choose to go down, be sure to go for an oil with a high smoke point such as peanut or grapeseed oils. If your machine's instructions indicate that you can, try beef dripping, but this will become solid when cold so may be very difficult to clean out.

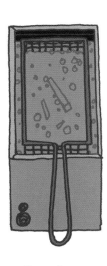

Open fryers   Closed fryers

Open fryers are usually electric and the simplest to work. Buy one that has an adjustable temperature dial so you can set it for the correct temperature for the oil you're using. Using too much or too little oil is a mistake, because too little will mean that the oil will drop in temperature when you add the food to be fried, and too much oil makes the chance of oil spilling over a greater risk. In a family environment, the danger of someone touching the outer casing of a fryer is greater, and as oil is far hotter than the boiling point of water – even contact with the heated container can give severe burns – it may be better to use a closed fryer with insulated sides. The other advantages of closed fryers are that the heated air is vented through a filter which reduces any smells for the oil/cooking, and that spitting oil is contained within the fryer. If the fryer has a window in the lid you can also check the progress of the frying without having to open it.

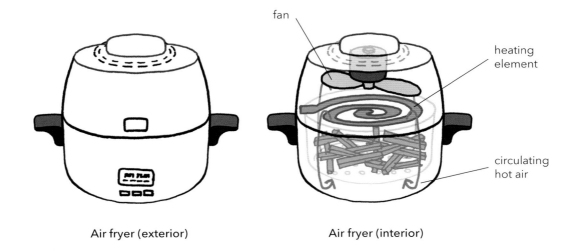

fan

heating element

circulating hot air

Air fryer (exterior)   Air fryer (interior)

Air fryers work by cooking food with very hot air that circulates around the container. A small amount of fat can be added to the food to add flavour, but in most cases if you were to cook chips (fries) the results would taste more like oven chips than deep-fried chips. Air frying is not limited to potatoes, and a wide range of foods can be cooked with these devices. The positive points are largely safety and health-related because you are not heating a large amount of flammable fats, and you will also be consuming less of these fats.

DOUGHNUT MAKERS

Traditionally, doughnuts are deep fried, and this can be done with open or closed fryers, but there are now dedicated doughnut makers that are much more like waffle makers. You oil the surface of both the base and lid, and then pour a thick batter into recesses in the base, close the lids and wait. The results are more like a lightly fried cake than a doughnut, but they can be rather good…

STEAMERS

Steaming food has a number of advantages. As the food is not immersed in a liquid it doesn't diffuse away any flavour or nutrients, and no fat is added in the process. With delicately flavoured foods, it will preserve the flavour better than most other methods. Extra flavourings can be added to the water the food is to be steamed in.

 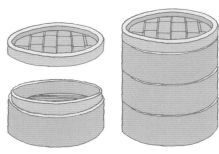 

There are a few types of steamer, and these include steaming pans, bamboo baskets, and freestanding electric steamers. Steaming pans work well and come with a number of levels that can be stacked as with the other forms of steamer. The advantage over the cheaper bamboo steamers is that you don't have to place anything under the food to avoid it sticking. Bamboo steamers are very cheap, and if you don't use one regularly, they are a good choice. If you do use one then either line the inside base with greaseproof paper or place the food on a heatproof dish in the base.

Electric steamers are useful and some even feature delayed timers so you can program them to have food ready at a specific time and start cooking when you are absent. On the downside, they are not usually that easy to clean (when compared with a pan that you can place in a dishwasher or easily hand-wash), and they also take up space.

FONDUE

RACLETTE

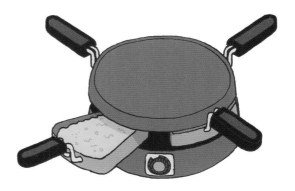

Fondue makers are largely a modern invention featuring a deep communal pot mounted over a gas flame, but fondue has been made since the end of the 17th century. However, the recipe was rather different and included wine and cheese. In the 1930s, Swiss cheese producers promoted the idea that fondue was a Swiss national dish as a way of selling more cheese. Gruyère cheese was expensive and was produced largely for the export market, but this didn't hinder the success of the campaign, and by the 1960s fondue sets were available across the world. To avoid the cheese separating it is best to add a little cornflour (corn starch). Chocolate fondue was invented to promote Toblerone chocolate in the 1960s.

The pot can also be used to heat oil or a broth that food can be dipped into to cook, which a method used in Japan and China and other parts of Asia.

Raclette is a particular cheese from Switzerland that is most commonly eaten when melted. It was originally melted and scraped from the whole cheese and served with potatoes and dried meats. This has become a sociable tradition as part of a shared meal, much like fondue. There are now electric machines involving several small pans that the cheese is placed into, which are mounted over heat to soften and cook the cheese.

ROTARY EVAPORATORS

The rotary evaporator is a form of distillation still that is used to extract the flavours of fresh foods. Whatever is to be distilled is placed in a flask (the source flask), which is then rotated over a temperature-controlled water bath, while a vacuum pump reduces the pressure. This allows boiling to occur at low temperatures (often below 40°C/104°F), and the vapour travels through the device and passes over a chilled 'condenser' where it collects as a liquid and drops down to be caught in another flask (the collection flask).

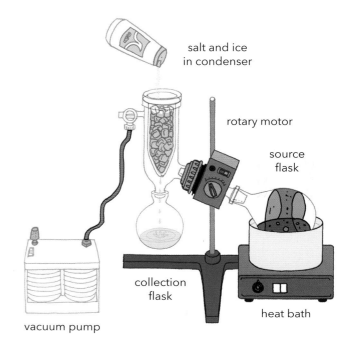

salt and ice in condenser

rotary motor

source flask

collection flask

heat bath

vacuum pump

FREEZE DRYERS

Freeze drying is a process that removes water from foods while leaving the fundamental structure intact. The food is first frozen and then put in a container that has a vacuum pump attached to it. The food defrosts, but as it is in a vacuum, the water doesn't turn to a liquid, but a vapour. This reduces the damage to the structure of the food, as well as allowing the food to become much drier than under normal pressure. The food can then be stored for long periods, and then rehydrated or used dry (this can be in its dried-out shape or ground into a powder). Foods rich in sugar are hard to dry even with this process as the sugars are hydroscopic (i.e. they hold onto water).

The process does need some heat for the frozen food to 'sublimate' off the water, and this is taken through the container walls, or in some cases from heat either transmitted from elements by conduction or through infrared lamps by radiation, as heat cannot travel through the vacuum by convection.

CENTRIFUGE

Centrifuges spin objects around rapidly, generating forces of around 4,000 times normal gravity, and in some very heavy-duty centrifuges in excess of 55,000 'G'. This has the effect of separating out foodstuffs into component layers, so a finely blended food may separate out into fats, cellulose mass, water, and water-soluble chemicals, for example. While only used in a very limited number of restaurant kitchens, centrifuges have been used in a number of food plants for many years.

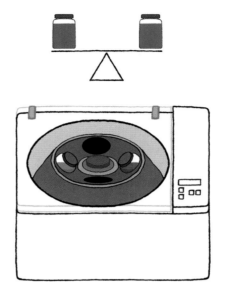

Because the weight is vastly increased while spinning the load in the centrifuge, it must be very carefully balanced to avoid causing stress damage to the machine or even destroying it.

BLAST CHILLER / SHOCK FREEZERS

These are powerful refrigeration units that can very rapidly cool and/or freeze foods. There are a number of advantages to this: taking hot food and chilling it rapidly doesn't allow much time for bacterial growth in the food as it passes through the 'danger zone' of temperatures for bacteria. The second advantage is that rapidly frozen foods have smaller ice crystals forming in them during the process of freezing. This reduces damage to the structure of the food and helps it maintain its texture. It also allows for the fast production of foods in a busy environment.

Some units are just blast chillers, while others have the function of shock freezing as well.

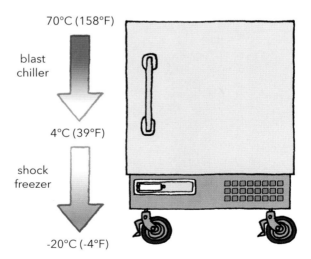

70°C (158°F)

blast chiller

4°C (39°F)

shock freezer

-20°C (-4°F)

FISH SCALER

While a lot of fish bought from shops has be de-scaled, if you have access to fresh fish, it is worth having a fish scaler to remove the scales as they are unpleasant to eat. The fish is held by the tail and the scaler is dragged up the body to the head until all the scales are removed and the fish should be turned over the complete both sides. Rinse the fish afterwards to wash scales.

RICERS & MASHERS

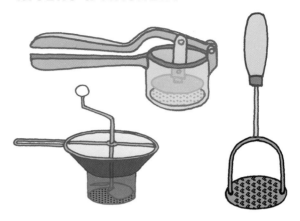

Ricers and mashers are useful when you want to produce a smooth mash for a dish or prepare food for very young children. The press-down ricer, or the masher are good for this but the rotating handled ricers are difficult to use and are limited.

TERRACOTTA BRICK

Variations of the terracotta 'brick' have been used for thousands of years, and are very good at keeping the food moist while cooking. The brick is soaked in water before filling with food and it's then placed in a cold oven and the heart turned on (to avoid breaking the terracotta with thermal shock). The moisture seeps out as steam as the food cooks but doesn't stop it from browning.

TAGINE

The original tagines are earthenware and used in fires to cook food. The cone shape collects any moisture that rises from the food and allows it to settle and fall back onto the food to keep it moist. They can be used in the oven but unless they are heated gently they can crack, so the earthenware are often used just to serve food cooked in another pot. You can now buy oven- and hob-safe tagines.

PASTA

Pasta has be prepared by hand for hundreds of years. The dough can be made on the table top and after 'resting' it is rolled out (for most pasta shapes, but not all). A table is better than a narrow work surface as the pasta is rolled out to a large single piece, using a very long roller (that is sometimes made from a broom handle). It is then cut to form different shapes. Sometimes it is formed by hand-rolling from thin strips. These thin can be made by using a 'guitar', which is a frame with wires strung across it that large pieces of flat pasta are laid onto before a roller is used to push them through the wire, which cuts the pasta into fine strips.

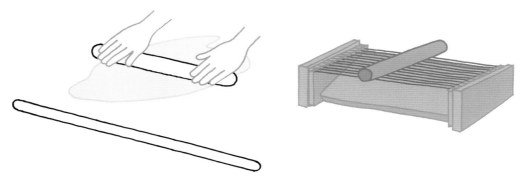

Hand-operated pasta machines can be used to form the dough into flat strips that are worked through the many rollers of the machine until the pasta becomes a smooth consistency and suitable thickness. Attachments on these machines can be used to reduce the wide, thin strip into thin strip pasta, such as linguine, or even shaped pasta.

Recently home electric pasta machines have become available that the ingredients are placed in and then the machine mixes, kneads, and finally extrudes through a 'die'. On commercial machines bronze is sometimes used to make the dies and this is often mentioned on the packaging the pasta comes in. The bronze die often leaves a slightly rough surface on the pasta that, when cooked, holds sauce well.

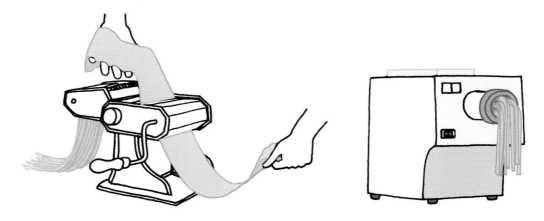

COOKING

PREP

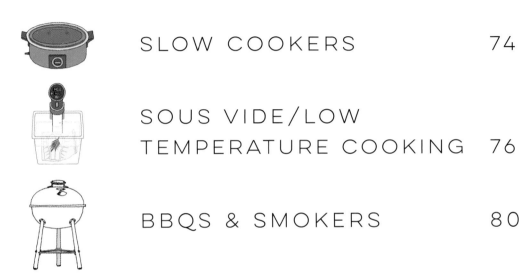

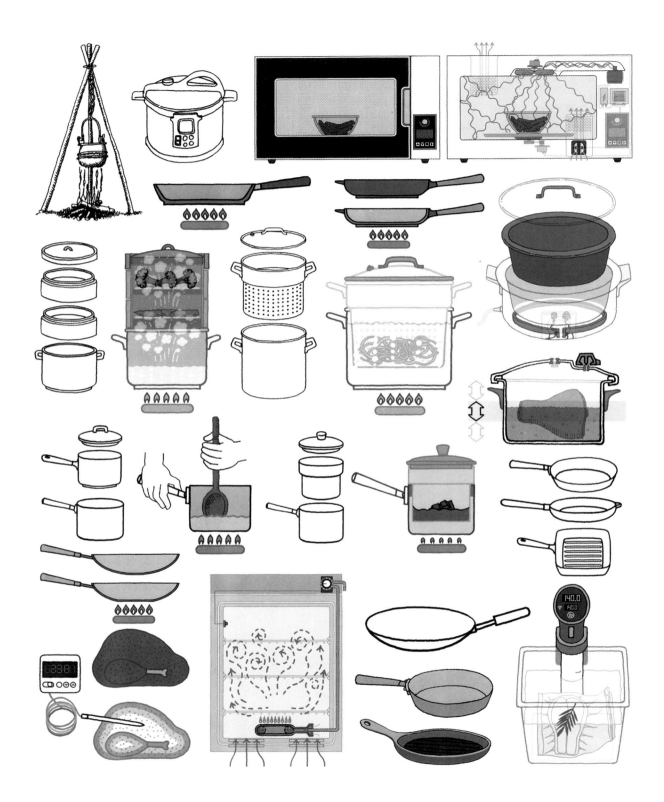

WHAT IS COOKING?

Cooking is part of culture and is sometimes seen as the craft or even art of food preparation. Technically 'cooking' can be described as the irreversible changing of foods by applying heat. With heat, the proteins and other large molecules in foods are altered and new molecules are formed. This can also happen in the presences of acids, alkalies, and enzymes (for example, citric acid in lime juice in the case of the dish ceviche 'cooks' the raw fish by altering its molecules, and enzymes from yeast allowing for the formation of gluten in bread). Heat can cause Maillard reactions and caramelization. Both of these processes form complex new chemicals that can brown the food and create new flavours. Maillard reactions happen in the presence of amino acids, while caramelization happens in presence of certain complex sugars, and causes them to breakdown into simpler sugars.

The process of cooking often makes the food more digestible, and therefore nutritious, as well as tasty, and often safer to digest by killing bacteria, and destroying some toxins.

OVENS & STOVES

Stoves originate from open fireplaces after humans settled from hunter-gatherer societies with the development of agriculture. Fireplaces became a fixed point in a home and soon started to evolve. Air was channelled in around the fire, stands to hold food while cooking became fixtures, pots started to be used as cooking containers, and people tried to vent the smoke away. In some cases the fire became enclosed and these were the earliest of stoves.

The ancient Egyptians, Chinese, Indians and the Romans all had stoves and/or ovens, and variations of these formed the basis of cooking until the Industrial Revolution. When metal started to be used for pots, the pots were positioned in structures over the fire or even placed in the fire with coals heaped over the lid.

Stoves (of various kinds) were much more common in countries where firewood was a rarity as it was more fuel efficient to cook with a stove than an open fire. Methods were developed to cook things quickly and with minimum fuel, hence food was often cut into small pieces before cooking (as with much traditional Chinese cooking where meat and vegetables are shredded before cooking).

In London in 1785, Count Romford set about developing a chimney that would burn fuel cleanly, and in doing so he eliminated the need for deep open fires. Cast-iron fireplaces became common and Count Romford then set about designing ovens to be set into the fireplace. This style of oven spread rapidly. By the late 19th century gas became available to homes and a gas cooker that eliminated the need to constantly stoke a fire slowly became popular. It was not long after this that the first electric ovens were developed. These took longer to become popular as electricity was not widely available and, where it was, it was expensive to use. Since those times there have been a wide range of developments in ovens, hobs, and stoves, including the microwave oven that appeared after discoveries while developing radar during the Second World War.

OVENS

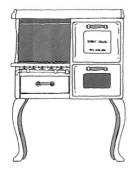

While cheaper to buy and run, many gas ovens are less flexible, and can cook food unevenly compared with electric ovens. Electric ovens may have additional elements and grills that can be combined to cook things in different styles, and generally heat the oven more evenly. This is further improved with fan-assisted ovens.

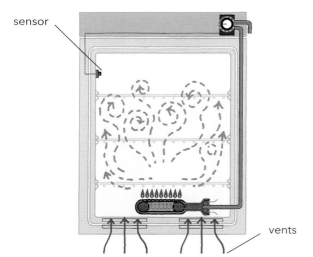

sensor

vents

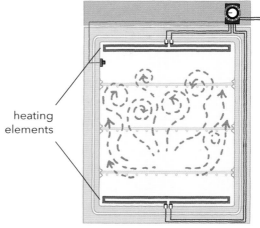

heating elements

GAS OVENS

Gas ovens usually have the burner at the bottom of the oven and have vents to allow fresh air (needed for burning) into the oven. The heat will rise so the temperature will vary within different positions within the oven. A sensor will regulate the temperature, based on the knob position.

ELECTRIC OVENS

Electric ovens regulate the temperature with a sensor in the oven (much like gas ovens, but as they don't need vents they heat the oven more evenly). Opening the door can drop the oven temperature a lot, and it may take quite a long time for the oven to reach the desired temperature again. So try to reduce the time the door is open. The displayed temperature may also not be accurate.

FAN OVENS & FAN-ASSISTED OVENS

A fan oven features a fan with a heating element mounted behind it. The oven heats up as soon as it is turned on. The fan mixes the air and causes the heat to reach most areas inside the oven much more equally. This makes the food cook faster at any given temperature setting for an oven, hence why cooking times for fan ovens are shorter. In ovens without a fan, the temperature in different parts of the oven can vary as much as 12°C (54°F) or more.

By contrast, fan-assisted ovens feature two heating elements, one at the top and one at the bottom, along with a fan in the rear. The time it takes to reach full temperature is the same as a standard oven, but they heat the food more efficiently, so cooking temperatures are usually lower.

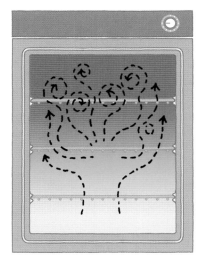

Standard oven

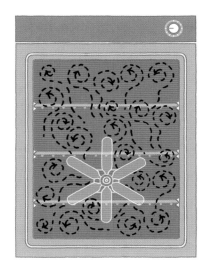

Fan oven

Note that it is dangerous to use hand rails on cookers to store towels or oven gloves. It can affect the airflow on some ovens and can be a fire hazard.

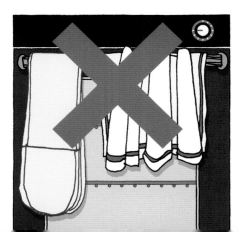

61

TEMPERATURE, THERMOMETERS & PROBES

Most ovens not only vary in temperature in different parts of the oven, but they also do not have accurate temperature controls and displays (this inaccuracy can be as large as +/-25°C/77°F). One of the cheapest and greatest improvements you can make to your cooking is to use an in-oven thermometer so you can correct for this.

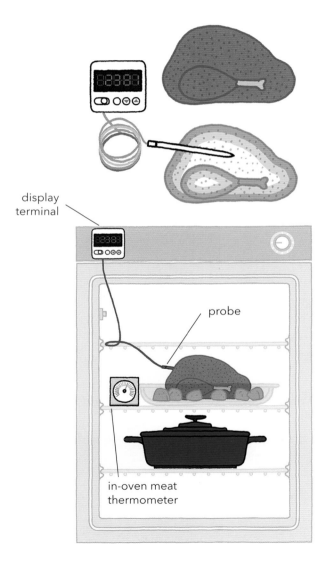

display terminal

probe

in-oven meat thermometer

Digital thermometers with probes will improve the control you have over what it is you are cooking, and they can be bought quite cheaply.

These are particularly useful for roasting joints of meat, because the 'doneness' is determined by the meat reaching a particular temperature. With some digital probes, you simply insert the probe into the thickest part of the meat to check how well the meat is cooked.

Some digital thermometers with probes are designed so the display terminal can sit outside of the oven, while the probe, attached by a heatproof cord, sits in position in the meat. This type of probe typically features an alarm so it will ring when the meat reaches a temperature that you have already pre-set.

GENERAL ADVICE

Roasts

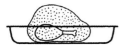

Select a pan somewhat larger than your joint of meat so that the juices can collect but do not steam the meat. If the pan is too large, the juices may dry out and burn. There are so many variations in terms of the size of the joint and the desired level of doneness, etc., but if you use a digital thermometer with a probe, it's fairly easy to achieve the result you were after. Pre-browning the joint and seasoning is well worth doing to maximize the flavour.

Stews

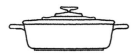

While stews and casseroles can be cooked on a hob, it is far easier to cook them in an oven, because this will avoid burning from the direct heating of the vessel. At a relatively low heat over a long period, even tough cuts of meat should soften nicely. Vegetarian dishes can involve much shorter cooking times than with meat, but if you are using soaked, uncooked kidney beans you should make sure they are boiled for at least 10 minutes to destroy the harmful toxins they contain.

Bread

Bread and its variations are cooked at high oven temperatures (often around 220°C/430°F), and the oven should be given plenty of time to warm up. Placing a tray of water in the base of the oven will produce steam that will vastly improve the quality of the bread's crust. Using a pizza stone or other baking stone will help bake the base of the loaf.

Cakes

Cake baking is more of a precise art than almost any other type of cooking. Use a good recipe, follow the process and quantities exactly, and use the right size of cake tin. The size of tin greatly affects the cooking time. The oven should be pre-heated and the cake mixture put into it as soon as its mixed. The temperature and cooking time are also important so use a good thermometer to check that the oven is actually at the temperature suggested. Also, avoid opening the door, until very close to the end of the cook time, when it can be tested.

HOBS

Price, convenience, and ease of cleaning are all factors that influence the choice of hob. Gas is still the choice of most commercial cooks because it responds quicker to being turned up or down, but induction hobs are becoming increasingly popular.

GAS HOBS

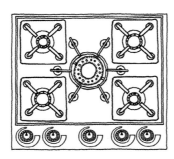

ELECTRIC RING HOBS

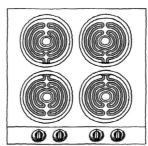

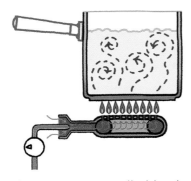

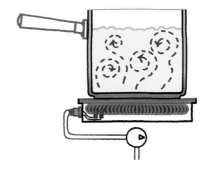

Gas burners are controlled by the knob which turns a tap. The gas travels up a pipe and through a jet. This jet pulls in air from a vent, which mixes with the gas before it ignites the burner ring.

ADVANTAGES
• Low- to medium-priced
• Fast to come up to/adjust heat
• Work well with woks

DISADVANTAGES
• Can be difficult to clean

Electric ring/plate-type hobs are controlled by a knob which allows varying amounts of electric current through to the element. This iron element is resistant to the current that flows through it and heats up.

ADVANTAGES
• Low priced
• Difficult to damage

DISADVANTAGES
• Difficult to clean, but also slow to react to adjustment of heat compared to other hobs.

GAS & ELECTRIC KNOBS

Gas   Electric

Gas hob knobs turn anti-clockwise, while electric knobs turn clockwise in a more intuitive way. This can seem strange when there is a mix of gas and electric on some cookers.

HALOGEN HOBS

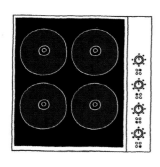

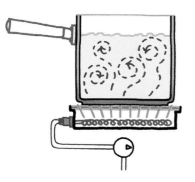

Halogen hobs use radiant heat. A knob controls the current flowing to a tungsten element, which heats until it glows, giving off infrared heat. The small amount of halogen stops the tungsten degrading.

ADVANTAGES
- Fast to come up to/adjust heat
- Easy to clean

DISADVANTAGES
- Mid- to high-priced

INDUCTION HOBS

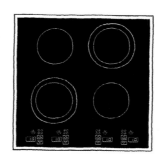

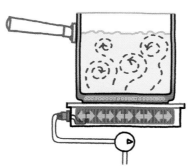

Induction hobs use a copper coil to generate a magnetic field. Only a pan with a magnetized base will heat up, making it very safe to use.

ADVANTAGES
- Fast to come up to/adjust heat
- Cheap and efficient to run
- Safe and easy to clean

DISADVANTAGES
- Mid- to high-priced
- Have to use steel-based pans

AGA & SIMILAR

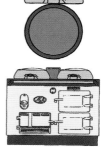

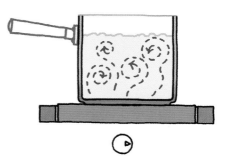

AGA cookers are slow to change temperature but hold temperature well due to their large thermal mass. Pans are heated almost solely by conduction, so it's important they have a very flat base.

ADVANTAGES
- Even heat distribution

DISADVANTAGES
- Very slow to come to temperature
- Requires flat-based pans

POTS & PANS

PAN MATERIALS

Copper heats quickly and evenly through the pan, but will lose heat quickly and therefore is not so good for searing/browning meat.

Aluminium is far cheaper than copper and distributes heat almost as well. A constant heat needs to be applied as the pan loses heat quickly when food is added.

Stainless steel is a good compromise as it heats reasonably quickly, and while it doesn't hold heat as well as iron, it will sear meat reasonably. Pre-heat the pan to distribute the heat evenly when cooking meat.

Iron is slow to heat and unless pre-heated properly, some areas will be hotter than others. Iron pans are porous so should not be soaked.

FRYING

Frying is also known as sautéing, and it usually involves some fat/oil. Avoid overloading the pan as this will steam the food and stop the food from browning. It is usually done on a medium to high heat.

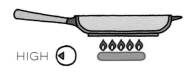

HIGH

If you are cooking steak, use a heavy pan if you have one, and pre-heat it until it is very hot. Dry the steak, and salt it quite heavily (most of the salt is lost in the pan). Then add a little oil, then the steak. Once the steak is in the pan, let it cook on one side without moving it about, for 2–3 minutes, then turn it over, and cook for a further 2–3 minutes. These instructions will achieve a medium-rare steak, assuming the steak is approximately 3cm (1¼ inches) thick.

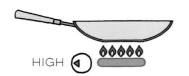

HIGH

Wok cooking is traditionally done with a thin iron pan over an intense heat, while the pan is kept moving to help spread the heat around the pan and to the food. Commercial Chinese kitchens use enormous gas burners to heat the pans, but home Chinese cookery is often done on hobs with little more heat than Western hobs. It is important to pre-heat the wok until it is very hot, so that the food fries/sears rather than steams. If you are not using gas you should use a flat-bottomed wok so it can generate heat from the hobs more efficiently.

Start by heating the wok, then add an oil that works well at a high heat (for example peanut or rapeseed oil), and when the oil starts to smoke, add the meat, fish, or tofu. Once it is starting to brown, add vegetables cut to similar sizes so they cook at an equal rate. While cooking keep the wok moving and stir the food to make sure it all cooks evenly.

PASTA

Purpose-made pasta pots are useful if you cook a lot of pasta. They come with an internal colander that allows the pasta to cook and then be removed from the water easily. Use plenty of water and salt. Heat until the water is boiling, add the pasta, and return to the boil. With dried pasta, it is worth testing the pasta by removing a piece and tasting and biting it. It should take 8–10 minutes for an al dente texture. With fresh pasta, the pasta will rise in the pan to the surface when its done.

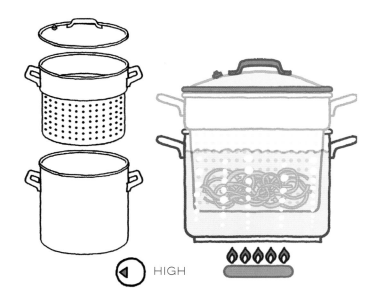

HIGH

SAUCES

Sauces such as a roux, béchamel, and cheese sauce are best done in a medium or small pan with a handle so that they can be held firmly when you have to mix them.

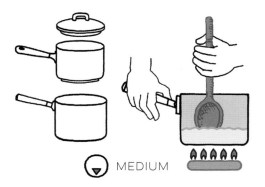

MEDIUM

BAIN-MARIE

Bain-marie pans are used to heat delicate foods that need gentle heating. They comprise an outer pan to hold water and an inner pan to hold the food. They are useful for melting chocolate, or for making sauces that don't need to be boiled, such as Hollandaise.

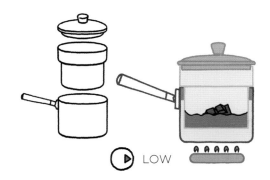

LOW

MICROWAVE OVENS

As well as being very convenient for reheating food quickly, microwave ovens actually do have a large number of uses in general cooking. But it is best to understand what exactly they can do so you can use one to its full potential.

Microwave ovens were first developed in 1945 after American engineer Percy Spencer discovered that microwaves (a form of electromagnetic radiation with wavelengths between 1mm/¹⁄₁₆ inch and 1 metre/3¼ feet) from a radar device caused a chocolate bar to heat up. Spencer filed a patent application on 8 October 1945, and the first microwave oven was used in a restaurant in Boston. The first commercially available product was called the Radarange and was sold in 1947. At 1.8 metres (5 ft 11 inches) in height and with a weight of 340 kg (750 lb) it looked rather different from modern versions.

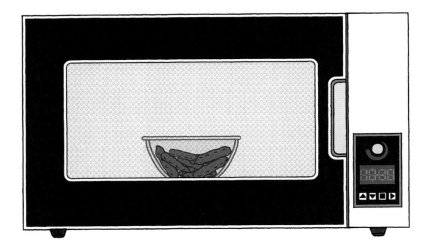

Some nutrients in food (such as vitamin C) break down with heat, but because a microwave cooks things quickly it preserves these nutrients better than many types of cooking. The word 'radiation' causes some people to fear microwaves, but it shouldn't – light, sound, and radio waves are all forms of radiation, after all. If a microwave oven is in good condition, it is a perfectly safe piece of equipment. The waves are approximately 12 cm (5 inches) and are generated by a device called the magnetron. The design of the microwave is such that the waves cannot escape.

The waves emitted in a microwave would heat a food unevenly, but two measures help the waves move evenly over the food. The most obvious one is the turntable which rotates the food. The second is through the fan-like device in the path of the waves that bounces them around the interior of the oven. Even so, small pieces of food can be missed by the waves, and there can be cool spots, which is why stirring the food regularly is important.

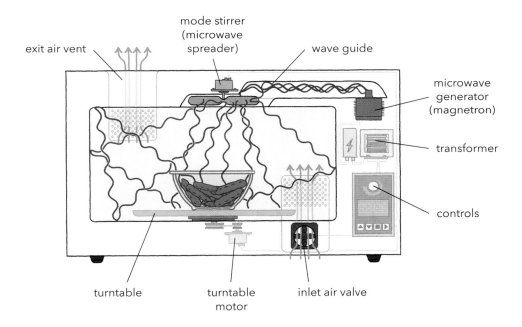

In most foods, it is the water, oils/fats that are heated by the waves. Dry foods don't heat well. Because food largely composed of water will be heated by the water present in the food, it will not brown, as it would with an oven that uses conduction, convection, or radiant heat. To get around this problem, manufacturers have combined these three types of heat with microwaves to form 'combination ovens'.

In the majority of models the controller acts as a timer, as well as switching the waves on and off during the cycle to adjust the amount of waves delivered to the food. If you listen to the microwave oven, you can often hear it turning on, running, and then switching out for periods over the course of cooking. If you turn down the power setting it will only turn on the actual microwaves for shorter periods, and space these cycles out. Newer models have started to use controls that actually adjust the amount of electricity supplied to the magnetron so it produces a constant output of waves at less density.

THE SHAPE & SIZE OF FOOD

When cooking with a microwave, the shape of the food is very important. The waves only pierce the food a little beyond the surface, and therefore large blocks of food will cook from the surface inwards. If the food is flat and relatively thin it will cook more equally. So large vegetables and joints of meat are better cut up.

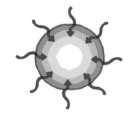 

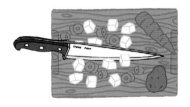

Chop food into similar-sized pieces so they cook at a similar rate.

Arrange food in rings so all the food gets cooked equally.

Cover bowls of food, and if using wrap, pierce holes in the wrap.

During the cooking, regularly stir the food so it spreads the heat evenly throughout the food.

Pierce foods with skins such as potatoes and sausages to stop them splitting or even possibly exploding.

To soften ice cream, use 10-second bursts at medium power and wait for 30 seconds between the bursts for the heat to distribute evenly.

You can dry herbs by placing them on a paper towel and heat them using a low setting until they are dry/brittle.

To make crisps, slice potatoes or other vegetables very finely, wash in fresh water, dry, then place on a paper towel and cook on a medium setting until they are crisp.

THINGS NOT TO DO WITH MICROWAVE OVENS

In normal operation, microwave ovens are safe, but there are a few things to avoid. Firstly, do not put any metal object or container in the microwave. This includes aluminium foil, take-away containers, crockery with metal gilding, cutlery, and pots and pans. Do not put whole eggs or grapes in as they can explode. Do not use plastic or foam containers unless they are microwave-safe. Things such as yogurt pots are not designed to be heated and some containers will melt, while others may release unpleasant chemicals into the food. Do not defrost frozen breast milk for babies as it may increase any bacterial contamination radically.

Use clingfilm (plastic wrap) to cover food but check it is microwave-safe. Cover food while microwaving as it may splatter, but avoid sealed containers as pressure may build up with heating. If you reheat drinks (not recommended), place a wooden spoon or stick in the cup to reduce the chance of it super-heating below the surface and boiling and splattering when you move or stir the drink.

!!! WARNING !!!

People have sometimes put old CDs and DVDs in microwave ovens to destroy them. In the process, it releases some extremely toxic fumes. These may contaminate the microwave, and certainly should not be breathed in. Do not do it.

PRESSURE COOKERS

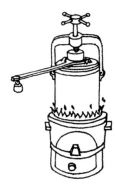

Pressure cookers were first invented in 1697 by Frenchman, Denis Papin. His device was called the 'Steam Digester' and he used it to extract fat from bones. Early pressure cookers were extremely dangerous but modern pressure cookers have many safety features and are completely safe unless damaged or abused. The modern pressure cooker started to become popular in the mid-20th century with the invention of various safety mechanisms.

The pressure cooker is essentially a large saucepan with an airtight, lockable lid. As the cooker heats up, the liquid inside forms steam, which makes the internal pressure rise. This raises the temperature beyond boiling point to around 115°C (240°F) which will help cook food faster. This can also kill some bacteria which can survive boiling. Specialized pressure cookers (known as autoclaves), which are used to sterilize items in hospitals, raise the temperature to 125°C (255°F) and higher. In America, large pressure cookers used for 'canning' achieve these higher temperatures to ensure they kill the bacterium *Clostridium botulinum* (which causes the potentially fatal illness botulism), which can develop in preserved foods.

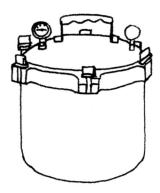

PRESSURE AT HIGH ALTITUDE

Atmospheric pressure falls the further away from sea level. The result is that at altitude, water boils at a lower temperature. This makes it difficult to cook some foods properly. So it is common for pressure cookers to be used at high altitudes, including on mountaineering expeditions. At Mount Everest's base camp, water boils at 82°C (180°F). By contrast, at Everest's summit, water would boil at only 71°C (160°F).

TYPES OF PRESSURE COOKERS

There are three types of pressure cooker commonly used in the home kitchen and these can be divided into 'venting', 'non-venting', and electric.

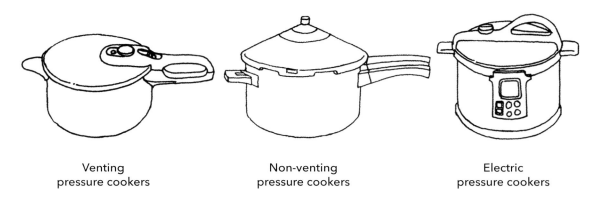

| Venting
pressure cookers | Non-venting
pressure cookers | Electric
pressure cookers |

Venting pressure cookers are the most common type and control temperature by venting steam through a valve. This valve is held in place by either weights or a spring.

Non-venting pressure cookers have to be 'set' more carefully but do not vent unless the temperature rises beyond what it is set for. While more expensive, the lack of venting preserves flavour.

Electric pressure cookers can be either of the two previous types but are automated and can be left to run programs for different foods/results. Often they run at slightly lower pressures than stove-top pressure cookers.

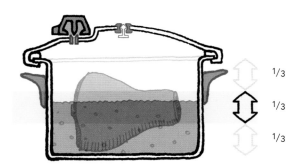

1/3

1/3

1/3

USING A PRESSURE COOKER SAFELY

Follow the manufacturer's instructions for general use and for information about how to clean it. Generally, it is advisable to fill the pressure cooker above one-third of the way up but below two thirds. Do not allow it to boil dry.

SLOW COOKERS

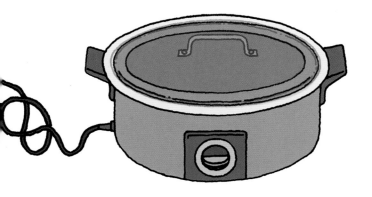

Slow cookers are economical to use and are very good at cooking food over a long period so that it is ready for a meal at a later time. This can be a few hours or over the course of the day so they can be used and left to cook while you are out to work. The temperature is below boiling and as they have quite a tight-fitting lid, the liquid in the dish does not dissipate, hence there is often the need to thicken the liquid to make a sauce. It is therefore better not to add too much liquid.

PARTS OF A SLOW COOKER

Slow cookers have three main parts: the base which contains the heater, a temperature-measuring sensor, and a controller. This controller can usually be used to set a program and/or time for the cooker to run for. Most programs run hot for the first part of the program (so as to reduce any bacterial growth from the start), and then reduce the temperature for the rest of the program time.

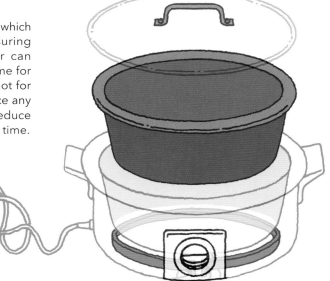

USING A SLOW COOKER

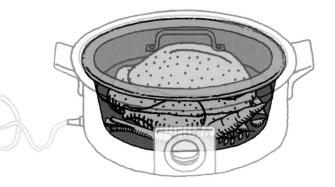

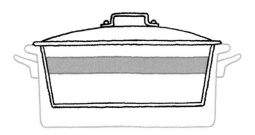

The dish should be between half and three-quarters full.

Slow cookers are useful for many types of dish. There are a few valuable pieces of advice to bear in mind, though. Firstly, it is necessary to pre-brown meats before adding them to the pot. Use less liquid than is specified by recipes for casseroles or curries because the liquid will not reduce. Also, make sure any herbs are below the surface of the liquid so that the flavour can permeate the dish. Vegetables should be added in quite large pieces so they do not break down too much.

When preparing any meat for slow cookers, note that you do not need to have much fat for the process. Cheap and tough cuts of meat are often well suited for a slow cooker because the long cooking time breaks down the structure of the meat, often producing very succulent and flavoursome meat.

Cuts that are particularly cheap and good for slow-cooking include:

- chuck
- short rib
- pork shoulder
- lamb shins
- ox tail

GENERAL ADVICE

- spray or wipe the interior with oil before starting.
- place hard vegetables on the bottom and make sure they are covered with liquid.
- use salt sparingly and season before serving.
- defrost foods before you start using the cooker.

SOUS VIDE/LOW TEMPERATURE COOKING

Sous vide is the term for cooking food in a vacuum-sealed bag that is then heated in a temperature-controlled water bath. It is not always necessary to use a vacuum bag, though – you can use a ziplock bag or one with a neck clip, but make sure they are well-constructed. The advantages of cooking in this way is that you can achieve very precise results, with the food cooking both evenly and to the exact level you require. A lot of the chemical changes that happen in the cooking process happen at different temperatures below boiling point, so sous vide is good for this.

The downsides of this style of cooking are:

1 Safety. Bacteria are very active between 10–50°C (50–120°F), and may not be killed in a sous vide alone, therefore great care should be taken with hygiene, preparation, and the cooking itself to avoid problems.

2 Food will not brown using this technique so it is recommended to brown the food (particularly meats) before or afterwards to enrich the flavour and presentability.

The most common type of sous vide cookers are the heated tank-type, and the immersion circulator. The tank-type is usually a self-contained device with a water tank, heater, control unit, lid, and method for circulating water in the tank. The immersion circulator is a device you insert into a tub or pot of water. It provides the heat, as well as moving the water and heat about, and a control set-up for timing and maintaining the temperature.

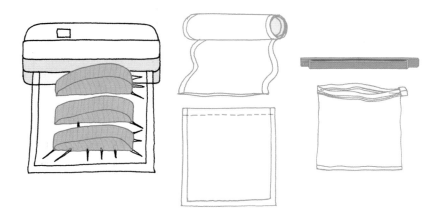

BASIC METHOD FOR THE IMMERSION CIRCULATOR

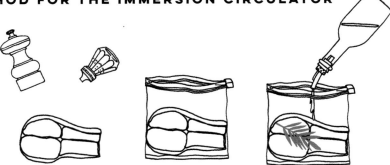

Place the meat in a bag with a little seasoning, any herbs, and some olive oil. Pre-heat the water in the container that is being used as the bath until it reaches the desired cooking temperature.

If using an ordinary bag, lower the bag slowly into the water so as to drive the air out, and seal the bag as the water reaches the top of the bag. Avoid getting water in the bag. Set the time and temperature on the immersion circulator and wait. Once the time has elapsed, take out the bag and empty it, so that you can use the juices if required to reduce for a sauce, and dry the meat before searing it in a hot pan to finish it. You can also use a blowtorch or blowtorch attachment such as the Searzal, to brown the meat.

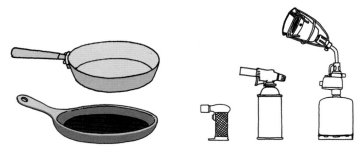

USEFUL TEMPERATURES

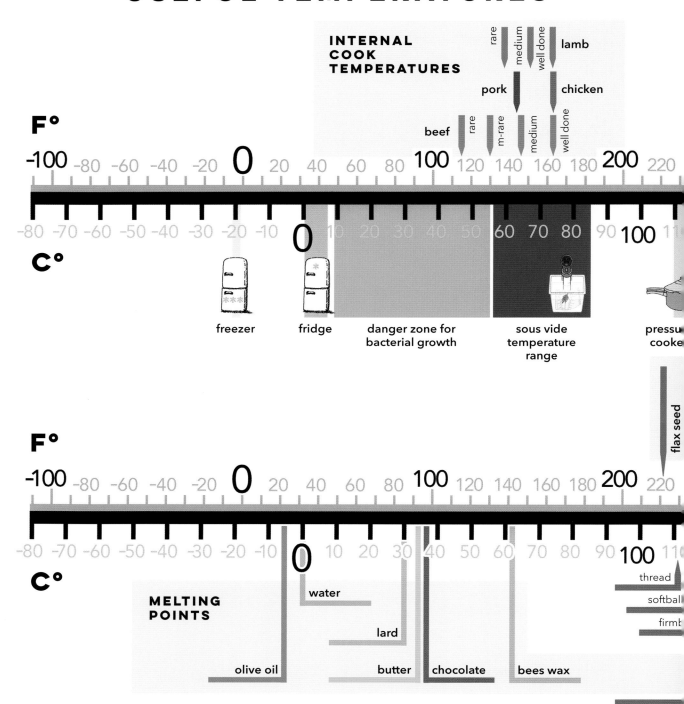

INTERNAL COOK TEMPERATURES

rare
medium
well done
lamb
pork
chicken
beef
rare
m-rare
medium
well done

F°
-100 -80 -60 -40 -20 0 20 40 60 80 100 120 140 160 180 200 220

-80 -70 -60 -50 -40 -30 -20 -10 0 10 20 30 40 50 60 70 80 90 100 110
C°

freezer
fridge
danger zone for bacterial growth
sous vide temperature range
pressure cooker

flax seed

F°
-100 -80 -60 -40 -20 0 20 40 60 80 100 120 140 160 180 200 220

-80 -70 -60 -50 -40 -30 -20 -10 0 10 20 30 40 50 60 70 80 90 100 110
C°

MELTING POINTS

water
lard
olive oil
butter
chocolate
bees wax

thread
softball
firmball

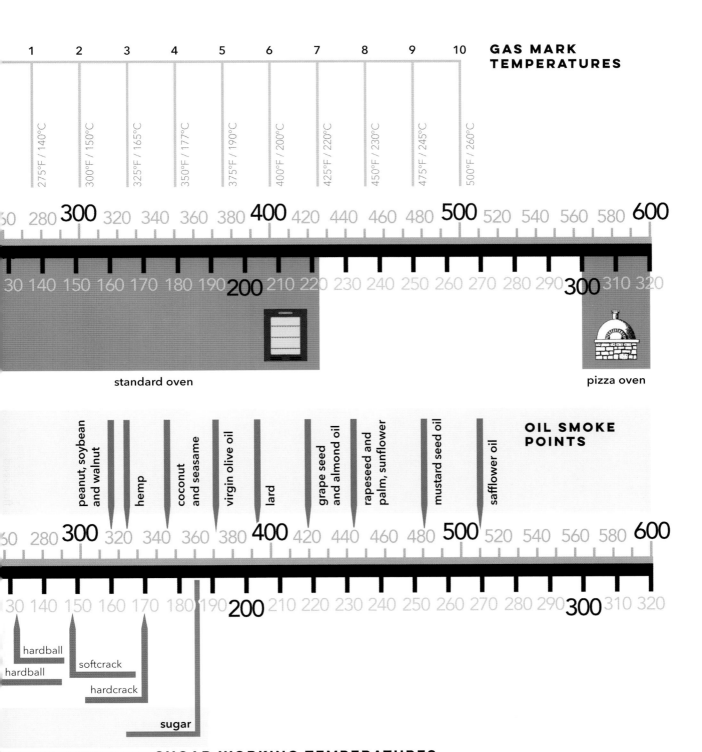

GAS MARK
TEMPERATURES

1 2 3 4 5 6 7 8 9 10

275°F / 140°C
300°F / 150°C
325°F / 165°C
350°F / 177°C
375°F / 190°C
400°F / 200°C
425°F / 220°C
450°F / 230°C
475°F / 245°C
500°F / 260°C

260 280 **300** 320 340 360 380 **400** 420 440 460 480 **500** 520 540 560 580 **600**

130 140 150 160 170 180 190 **200** 210 220 230 240 250 260 270 280 290 **300** 310 320

standard oven

pizza oven

OIL SMOKE POINTS

peanut, soybean and walnut

hemp

coconut and seasame

virgin olive oil

lard

grape seed and almond oil

rapeseed and palm, sunflower

mustard seed oil

safflower oil

260 280 **300** 320 340 360 380 **400** 420 440 460 480 **500** 520 540 560 580 **600**

130 140 150 160 170 180 190 **200** 210 220 230 240 250 260 270 280 290 **300** 310 320

hardball

hardball

softcrack

hardcrack

sugar

SUGAR WORKING TEMPERATURES

79

BBQS & SMOKERS

BBQs come in various types, but the most common is fired by charcoal. The oxygen in air burns in combination with the charcoal, and after an initial fast burn of impurities, the burning slows and gives a long heat that is most useful for cooking. Three types of heat do the cooking: 1) Radiant heat (infrared rays that are given out by the charcoal); 2) Convection heat (the heat transmitted in the gases that rise from the charcoal and make contact with the food); and 3) Conducted heat (the heat that collects in the grill that the food is sitting on, and then passes by direct contact with the food).

CHARCOAL BBQS

The major problem with BBQ cooking is temperature control. The charcoal is very hot and gives out a lot of radiant heat. If the food is too close it will cook rapidly on the outside before the inside of the food has had time to cook. Raising the food above the charcoal will slow the radiant cooking, and allow for more even heating of the food. Less charcoal will also work but may need more fuel before the food is ready. Placing the lid on the BBQ also helps as the smoke will block the rays of heat and slow the cooking as well as allowing greater transfer of flavour from the smoke.

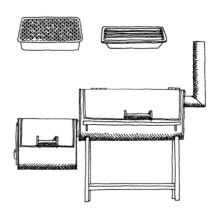

Lump charcoal   Briquettes   Binchōtan   Coconut shell charcoal

There are several types of charcoal for barbecuing. The most common are lump and briquettes. Lump is basic charcoal comprising wood that has been heated in a sealed environment so it is dried and chemically changes but doesn't burn (oxidize). It contains chemicals that vaporize during burning and flavour the food. Briquettes are made from a mix of wood shavings, dust, coal, and some binding chemicals. They may burn for longer and more evenly but may also flavour the food in a less pleasant way, particularly when first lit and before they are glowing red. The Japanese make a very refined charcoal called Binchōtan that is used in hibachi grills, particularly for cooking yakitori. It is very expensive and flavour-free. In Asia, the charcoaling process is used on coconut shells, and this is often used to cook street food such as satay.

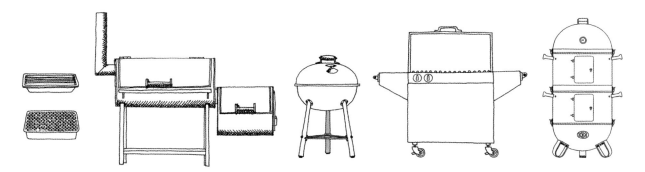

The flavour of food cooked by BBQ is a result of browning (creating more complex compounds with more flavours), and by chemicals in the smoke from the burnt fuel. Different charcoals will add different flavours, as will chips of wood, such as oak or hickory chips.

Air is drawn up from below and after passing the burning coal, it carries heat to the food above. This is called 'convection'. 'Radiant' heat travels like light from the glowing charcoal. 'Conductive' heat passes by direct contact from the grill to the food.

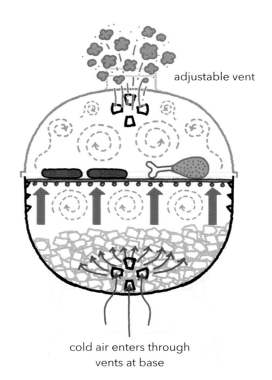

adjustable vent

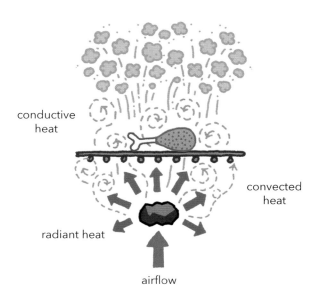

conductive heat

convected heat

radiant heat

airflow

cold air enters through vents at base

Placing the lid on the BBQ will slow the airflow and therefore the rate at which the charcoal burns. It will also reduce radiant heat and conductive heat because smoke will block the rays of heat to the food and grill. On many BBQs, there are adjustable vents on the base and lid so you can further control this. A gentler heat will allow the interior of the food to cook without burning the exterior, and also increase the smokey taste.

LIGHTING A CHARCOAL BBQ

Starting a charcoal BBQ can be done in many ways. Perhaps the simplest way is with the prepared bags that contain charcoal and a starter gel. These bags are ignited in the BBQ and the charcoal is lit by the combination of the gel and the burning bag.

Lighting fluid or gels are very common. These are often petroleum-based and should be allowed to burn off before the food is ever allowed near the charcoal. Stack the charcoal in a pyramid and spray with the fluid, then light carefully. The fire will flare up, then die back down. After 30 minutes or so, the charcoal will glow white hot. It is then ready to use for cooking.

To use solid firelighters, place a couple in the BBQ and arrange a pyramid of charcoal on top of them. Carefully light the firelighters and check that the charcoal catches.

If you are using a 'chimney starter', place a couple of firelighters on a heatproof surface (ideally a BBQ grill) and place the chimney on top. Fill the upper part of the chimney with charcoal. Light the firelighters. Once the charcoal is burning well, tip the charcoal carefully into the base of the BBQ.

GAS BBQS

Gas BBQs are quick to start up, offer easy temperature control, are often easier to cook evenly on, and some have multiple burners so you can have areas of different temperature for cooking different foods. They will not add any charcoal flavour but some allow drippings from the food to collect, carbonize, and create smoke to help provide some flavour.

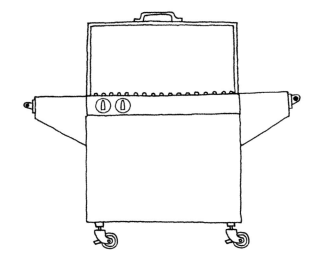

HOT SMOKERS VS COLD SMOKERS

Cold smoking is the process of flavouring food by passing smoke over it, while keeping the food below a temperature where it would cook (20–30°C/68–86°F). Hot smoking involves flavouring with smoke at temperatures where the food does cook (above 50°C/120°F and below 82°C/180°F). Above 82°C (180°F), the process is call 'smoke roasting'.

At cold smoking temperatures, bacteria can grow very quickly and make the food dangerous, so food should be quickly smoked and then cooked immediately. This can be done with an inexpensive smoking gun. Hot smoking is much safer as you are cooking the food at temperatures similar to low temperature/sous vide cooking, and this can kill bacteria.

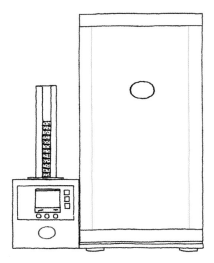

SMOKING MACHINES

Smoking machines are quite expensive but some can safely perform both hot and cold smoking. The most convenient machines use solid briquettes containing different woods so you can tailor the flavour. The internal temperature, the quantity of smoke, and the duration can be programmed by some machines, allowing you to smoke a wide range of foods.

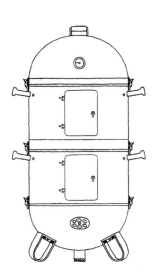

HOT SMOKING IN A BBQ

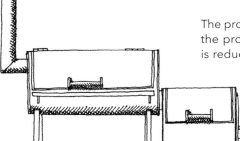

The process will vary a little from BBQ to BBQ, but the process is very similar in all BBQs. The heat is reduced or the food is kept away from intense heat and then wood chips or soaked, flavoured wood pellets are placed on or about the charcoal so smoke is slowly released over a long period. Heat and smoke are adjusted for maximum effect. Some BBQs have two or more chambers where the heat and smoke are kept separate before being allowed to flow into the chamber containing the food.

PIZZA OVENS

Pizza is a variation of flat breads, which are some of the oldest forms of bread known, traceable at least 3,000 years back to Sumerian culture, even though they are generally thought of as Italian. There are many variations of flat breads with toppings that can be found around the Mediterranean.

The wood-fired pizza oven has evolved little from traditional ancient ovens, with only the chimney design showing any developments. The oven is filled with wood which is set alight. Air is drawn in through the entrance of the oven, which is used in the combustion of the wood, and the heated gases rise and circulate around the oven, before being drawn up the chimney. The fire slowly raises the temperature of the stonework of the oven. Old large ovens could take a day or more to build up to temperature. Once the oven is hot enough, the ash and remaining wood are cleared to make an area for the food to cook on, and the food is placed in the oven. The temperature far exceeds a home oven (400°C/750°F, compared with 250°C/480°F for a home oven).

It is not just the actual temperature in the oven that affects the cooking, but the way that the heat is delivered to the pizza. Wood-fired ovens deliver heat in three ways:

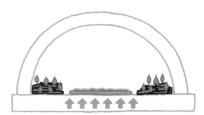

Conduction – heat that transfers to the pizza by direct contact with the surface of the oven.

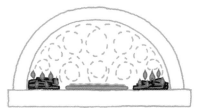

Convection – heat from the air and gas mix that circulates in the oven.

Radiation – infrared energy that travels like light from the burning fuel, and very hot oven walls.

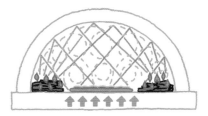

The result is a combination that produces a very particular and fine result with pizzas.

ELECTRIC PIZZA OVENS

Electric pizza ovens also use a combination of heating methods by using exposed heating elements that give out infrared radiation that heat both the air and heavy ceramic tiles in the oven as well as directly heating the food.

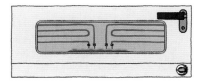 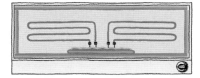

MAKING PIZZA AT HOME

Home ovens almost entirely heat the food by convection, which can be disturbed by opening the door. To best simulate a real pizza oven, the home oven has to be turned up to full heat, and used with a pre-heated block of stone or metal, or heavy pan to add conducted heat to the base of your pizza. Pizza stones and thick steel sheets can be bought that are designed for this purpose. Some ovens also have grills built in that can be used while the oven is on. This will add radiant (infra-red) heat, to further help achieve a well-cooked pizza.

Pizza stones and steel plates can greatly improve the quality of your pizza. They should be pre-heated in the oven, and the prepared pizza slid onto them at the time of cooking.

HOME COOKING METHOD

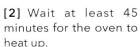 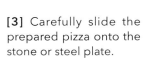

[1] Place the pizza stone or steel plate in the oven and turn the heat to full.

[2] Wait at least 45 minutes for the oven to heat up.

[3] Carefully slide the prepared pizza onto the stone or steel plate.

[4] Watch the pizza carefully and remove and serve when ready.

ICE CREAM & FROZEN DESSERTS

Ices have a long history and some of the earliest were made in China and Persia. For a long time they were made by mixing or ice or snow (which was often stockpiled in special buildings during the winter) with fruit and other ingredients. In the 17th century it was discovered in Venice, Italy that mixing salts with ice caused the temperature of the mixture to drop, and this could be used to cool a dessert in a container submerged in the mixture. This allowed new types of iced dessert, and these spread across Europe and the rest of the world.

FROZEN DESSERTS

SORBET

Sorbet is usually a mixed rather than whipped frozen dessert that is denser than ice cream and usually dairy-free. Alcohol is often used as a flavouring but this also lowers the freezing point and makes for a softer, smoother texture.

GRANITA

Granita is very much the same formulation as a sorbet, but the texture is coarse because in the process of making it, the liquid freezes and is then repeatedly broken up, until it is a grainy crystal texture.

SHERBET

Sherbet (from which the word sorbet is derived) was originally an Arabian recipe for a chilled fruit drink that might be sweetened. It is now usually much like a sorbet but often contains a low percentage of milk (around 3%). It may contain egg whites, and/or gelatine.

GELATO

Gelato was an Italian invention and the modern style of gelato usually has more dairy than a sherbet. It uses milk rather than cream, so the final fat content is usually 3–7%. Gelato is often made fresh in the best parlours, and held and served at a higher temperature than ice cream (-8 to -10°C/18 to14°F) rather than -14 to -20°C/7 to -4°F). It is denser than ice cream because it contains less air.

SOFT SERVE

Soft-serve ice cream is only available from commercial machines as the process cannot be replicated without the right equipment. Large amounts of air are mixed with ingredients that contain strong stabilizers to hold the ice cream/air mixture together. It is served at a higher temperature than harder ice creams and as a result less sugar is needed. Most of them are made from cheap pasteurized mixes.

ICE CREAM

Ice cream is used to describe many things but in most good recipes, 'ice cream' contains 7–10% dairy fat. It is churned to gather air into the mix as it freezes to maintain a good texture, and the faster it freezes the smaller the ice crystals and therefore the smoother the texture.

PREMIUM ICE CREAM

Premium Ice Cream is the name given to ice cream made with higher fat contents and less air in the mix. It is therefore often more expensive. This label is used in a number of countries and is a useful way to define what you're buying.

SUPER PREMIUM ICE CREAM

Super Premium Ice Cream has a high fat content (it can be over 20%). It also has a low air content and will use high-quality ingredients. Few home recipes are labelled Super Premium, but if a commercial ice cream is labelled as Super Premium expect it to be very creamy.

PASTEURIZATION

Pasteurization is the process of heating (but not boiling) and rapidly cooling food to kill bacteria and make food safe to eat. It lengthens the safe period that the food can be kept for. The reason it is rapidly cooled is so that it passes through the temperature range where bacteria grow quickly (the 'danger zone'), to a temperature where many of them are killed. This process is particularly important with dairy-based ice creams which can then be improved by ageing them in the fridge before freezing. The reason that pasteurization has advantages over boiling is that at higher temperatures the proteins in the milk are affected which in turn negatively affects flavour and texture (this is the reason that you avoid boiling the milk when foaming and steaming milk for coffee).

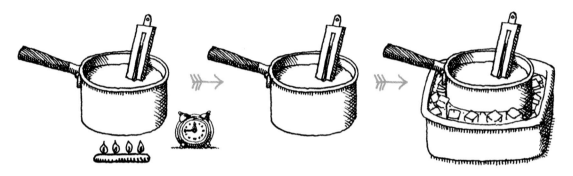

[1] Heat the mix until it reaches 83°C (181°F) and hold it at this temperature for at least 5 minutes.

[2] Take the pan off the heat and let it stand for 20 minutes to cool.

[3] Place the pan in a bowl of ice and water, then wait until the pan is below 10°C (50°F).

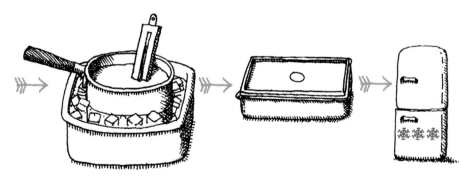

[4] Once cool, transfer to an ice-cream machine, or if you wish to age the mix, transfer it to a suitable container, and place in the fridge. The ageing process will take between eight and 16 hours. Ageing allows flavours to develop throughout the ice cream, and enables fats in the mixture to form larger crystal structures. This will enable the ice cream to hold more air and give it a smoother texture. This is particularly important with non-industrial ice cream making because domestic machines rarely have the ability to add much air.

ICE-CREAM MACHINES

Home ice-cream machines are not as powerful as commercial machines and have limited cooling power. This is important as the smoothness of ice cream is dependent on the size of the ice particles, and that is affected by the freezing time – the shorter the freeze time, the smaller the particles. So first pre-chill the mixture, or, in the case of refrigerated machines, run them empty until the mechanism is cold before adding the mix. The make-up of ice cream/sorbet mix also has an effect on the freezing, with high levels of sugar or alcohol needing longer chilling, so avoid recipes high in these.

HAND-CRANKED MACHINES

Salt and ice is one of the oldest methods still in use for making ice cream, and it still works extremely well. The cooling power of the mix is very effective and often more so than domestic machines. The downside is the amount of ice, salt, and human effort needed mixing (electric versions of salt and ice machines are available).

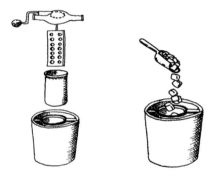

[1] Dissemble the machine, then put some ice in the bucket.

[2] Half-fill the mix container with your mix, then place the container in the bucket.

[3] Fill around the container with alternate layers of ice and salt. Fit the beater in place.

[4] Start mixing. Once the mix has thickened and increased in volume, it is ready to serve.

PRE-FREEZE MACHINES

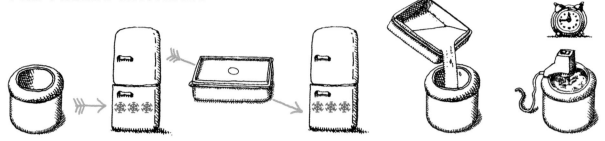

[1] Put the mix in the fridge and the freeze container from the machine in the freezer overnight. About an hour before you want to make the ice cream, transfer the mix from the fridge to the freezer.

[2] Pour the mix into the container, assemble the machine, and turn on. Check on progress; it is 'done' when the volume has increased and the texture is as thick as whipped cream but heavier.

REFRIGERATED MACHINES

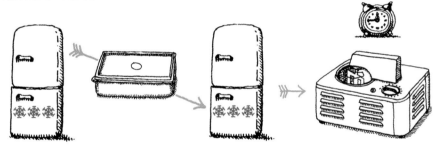

[1] About an hour before making the ice cream, transfer the mix from the fridge to the freezer.

[2] Turn on and run the machine empty about 15 minutes before adding the mix.

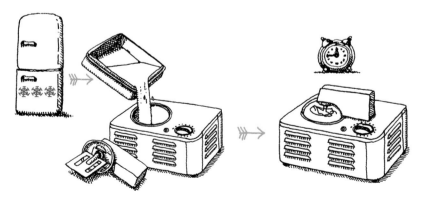

[3] Turn off the machine, add the mix from the freezer, then switch the machine back on.

[4] It's ready when the volume has increased and the texture is as thick as whipped cream but heavier.

FREEZING

GRANITA

Granita is the simplest of all ices to make.

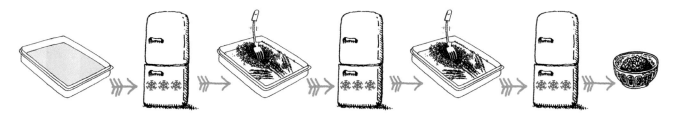

[1] After making your granita mix, allow it to cool and place it in a large, shallow container, and then put it in the freezer.

[2] Check it every half hour; once it starts to freeze, break up the ice and replace in the freezer.

[3] Start checking as it freezes more quickly and repeat the breaking up of the crystals until it has the texture you require.

ICE CREAM, SORBET & GELATO BY HAND

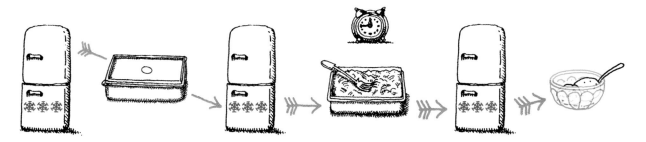

A similar method to the one above can be used for almost any ice cream, sorbet, or gelato. If you want to end up with a smooth texture, repeat the mixing and breaking up of the ice crystals more often and until the mix is fairly hard. The volume of mix, how much you pre-cool it, and how much sugar are in the mix will all affect how long it takes to freeze.

When your ice cream is ready, you can serve it or you can harden it more in the freezer. Make sure it is in a suitable container, cover it to avoid spoilage from the air, and place it in the freezer.

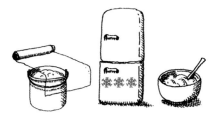

BAG METHOD

This works well and can be quicker than a commercial machine. It does take quite a lot of ice and salt, good strong plastic bags, and a certain amount of effort. Do use a thick towel as it can get very, very cold.

[1] Pour the cooled mixture into a strong foodsafe plastic bag, and seal it.

[2] Add ice to a second foodsafe plastic bag and about one-quarter as much salt.

[3] Place the first bag into the second bag and seal it.

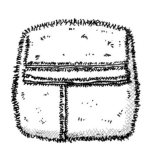

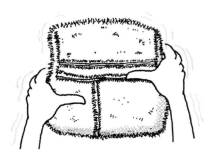

[4] Wrap the bags in a large, thick towel. Salt and ice can drop as low as -18°C (-4°F), so wear gloves or add a second towel if necessary.

[5] Gently massage the inner bag through the towel and outer bag.

[6] Once the mix has become firm (but not solid) take out the inner bag, wipe off any salt, and serve.

LOLLIES, POPSICLES & PALETAS

  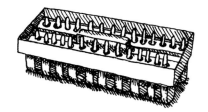

Known as popsicles in the USA, lollies in the UK, and paletas in Central America, these frozen desserts on a stick have been about for at least 100 years, and are now consumed around the world. Flavours vary from culture to culture. They are extremely simple to make and in some cultures they are mostly homemade and even sold from the front doorstep (as they are in parts of Mexico).

It is perfectly possible to make them at home without commercial moulds by using cleaned disposable containers or anything that is safe to let ice form in. Ceramics should be avoided as they may crack as ice expands.

When releasing them from the mould after freezing, you can dip the outside of the moulding in tepid water but avoid hot water as this may melt things too much. If you wish to add things in the moulds you can experiment, but consider allowing layers to freeze hard before adding further layers. Pre-chill the new layer to avoid melting the frozen layer. Fruit pieces and pulps can be used as well as juices, and after freezing you can add texture with a chocolate coating (melt chocolate and add 5% peanut or coconut oil to stop the coating being too brittle).

Alcohol will reduce the freezing temperature and may separate out from any other liquid, so it is best avoided above very small amounts.

MOULDED ICES

Moulded ices were very popular for hundreds of years, and elaborate moulds are still available, but you can also use simple bowls. They are often made of plastic, aluminium, copper, silicone, or glass, but avoid using glass moulds as they are often difficult to release the dessert from. In Victorian times, they were often greased to avoid this problem.

 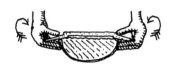

To release the moulded shape, dip the outside of the mould in tepid water and then invert. You can avoid the shape dropping straight out of the mould and breaking by placing a lid or plate onto the mould before inverting.

-20°C (-4°F) (very hard)   -15°C (5°F) (hard)   -8°C (17°F) (melting)   outer shell   soft interior filling

Large frozen desserts will be slower on the inside to warm than the outside, so when you try to cut it, it may be too hard and cold on the interior while the outside is melting. To avoid this situation you can cast the mould with an outer shell, then a softer interior filling, (or something that has a higher sugar content, or a dash of alcohol) so it will all soften at the same rate. To do this you can use two moulds with one leaving the space for the second inner dessert mix to be added after the first outer shell layer has frozen. You can also fill a frozen shell with foam from a whipper and let that harden in the freezer.

DRINKS

DRINKS

WATER & FILTRATION

There are a few aspects to consider when using water in drinks, or in the making of food: flavour, mineral content, safety, and expense.

Flavour is affected by minerals contained in the water, and in the case of tap water, by the main chemical used to sanitize it – chlorine. Minerals in the water may also interact with things mixed with the water (such as when making tea or coffee).

Tap water in Britain is nearly always safe to drink, but mineral levels very much depend on local supply and variations in chlorine levels, so flavour and suitability for use in making drinks may vary widely.

Boiled tap water will lose much of any chlorine taste it had from the tap, but will not affect the 'hardness' (see right) of the water.

Filter jugs can also remove chlorine and other tastes from tap water, but will not alter the mineral levels. Filters have a limited life and must be replaced regularly (check the manufacturer's instructions).

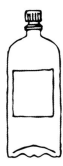

Cheaper bottled water is usually taken from the public supply, filtered and sometimes has minerals added. The mineral levels often work well in tea or coffee if tap water doesn't. It is often labelled as 'mineral water'.

Water labelled as 'spring water' is often more expensive and may have a particular taste due to the local minerals found in the rocks that the water passes through. Only a very few spring waters are naturally carbonated.

Plumbed-in filtration systems can remove chlorine and minerals. Filters have to be changed regularly, which can be expensive, but may reduce mineral build-up in kitchen equipment, which in turn may save money.

'SOFT' & 'HARD' WATER

'Soft' and 'hard' are used to describe the amount of minerals in the water. Soft has none to little, and hard has more. Very soft water is not that pleasant to drink because it can taste salty but the lack of minerals means that they cannot settle and build up as mineral deposits in pipework and kitchen appliances. Hard water may taste better but will have a detrimental affect on pipes and equipment, and also interacts with soap to produce sediments (scum). In very hard water areas it may be beneficial to fit a filtration system that deals with minerals to extend the life of your appliances. While hard water is not great for coffee machines, most coffee experts prefer a low level of minerals but not very low or no levels…

While stove-top kettles are still used in much of the world, electric kettles are now very popular in countries that use 220/240 volt electric power, as 110 volt power is not efficient at heating an electric kettle quickly. While the modern electric kettle is used to 'heat on demand', in Japan and the Far East, insulated kettles maintain water just a few degrees below boiling point and then boil that water almost instantly and supply it via a pump to a tap. These are very convenient.

'DE-SCALING' A KETTLE

Kettles that are filled with 'hard water' will over time build up limescale deposits that can eventually affect the efficiency with which the kettle heats up, and even possibly damage it. To remove the scale you can use a 1-to-1 mix of white vinegar and water. Let the mix soak in the kettle for an hour and then bring to the boil. After letting the mix cool, tip it out and then rinse the kettle throughly and wipe clean.

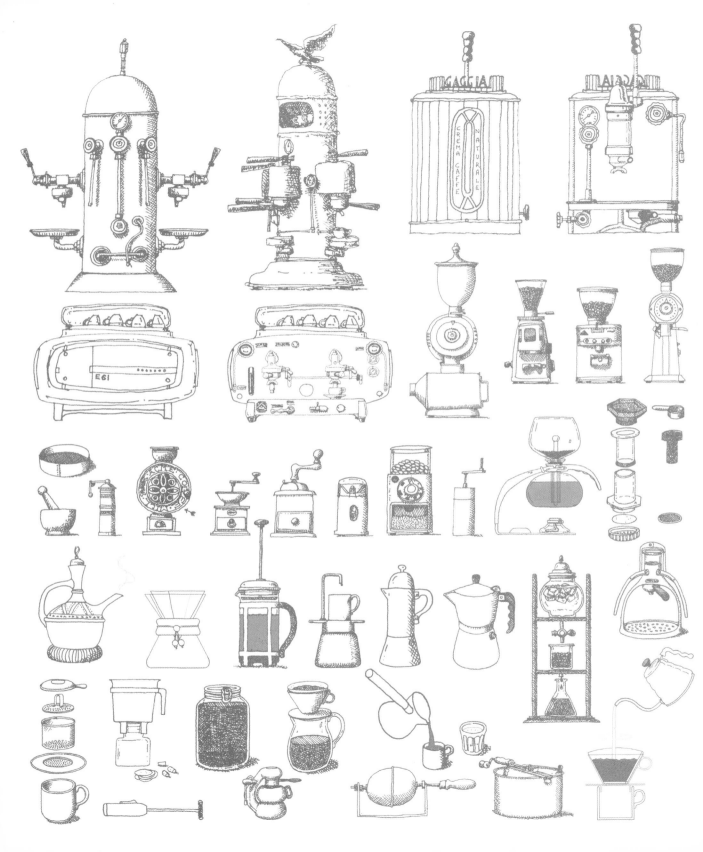

COFFEE

HISTORY

Coffee has been drunk in its home lands of the Yemen and Ethiopia for more than a thousand years, but it spread more widely through the Islamic world about 500 years ago. In about 1600, coffee arrived in Venice. At that time Venice was the major trading centre for many goods entering Europe from the rest of the world. Coffee then travelled across Europe and quickly became fashionable. It was taken to the new world of the Americas in about 1650, and in 1723 the French took coffee seedlings to Martinique where it grew well and started to spread through the Caribbean, and then Central and South America.

BIOLOGY

Coffee is a member of the Rubiaceae family of plants that also includes cinchona (from which quinine is extracted), and madder (the oldest source of red dye). There are about 25 coffee species but only two (Robusta and Arabica) are generally used for coffee production, though Liberica, and Dewevrei are grown in very small quantities. The coffee bean is the seed, and grows inside a berry that is sometimes dried and used to make a drink called Cascara, which is very high in caffeine. The beans form inside the berry, usually in pairs but in about 5% of cases a single bean forms and these are known as peaberries. Arabica, which is considered higher quality than Robusta, has two common sub-varieties (Typica and Bourbon) that form the basis of further breeding.

CHEMISTRY

The coffee bean before it is roasted is bitter in taste from the caffeine content. This is produced by the plant to repel insect and animal attack. The bean also contains a huge range of other related chemicals and when the bean is roasted the mix of the these chemicals produces a huge number of further chemicals. By the time the coffee drink is made there are over a thousand chemicals given off, but the main smell is derived from perhaps only a dozen detectable ones. As the coffee cools there is a process called retrogradation which means some chemicals reform. This is why coffee becomes more bitter as it cools, and shouldn't be reheated.

ROASTING COFFEE

Home roasting can be done with coffee roasting machines, hand-turned coffee roasters, popcorn makers, or basic kitchen equipment. You can use a heavy pan, but a certain amount of trial and error is needed. Select your beans for quality, and for the style of roast you want. The beans keep longer before roasting so it is better to roast in batches sufficient for no more than two weeks, and do this a couple of days before you need them to allow time for the beans to 'rest'. Carbon dioxide is generated within the beans during roasting which affects the flavour, brewing, and the 'bloom', but this dissipates in the resting period.

Set a hob ring to a medium heat, and remember that the beans roast a little after you remove the pan from the heat, so take it off just before it reaches the desired style.

USING A HAND OR ELECTRIC ROASTER

Turkish hand roaster

'Whirley Pop' roaster

Popcorn roaster

Home electric roasters

When coffee was first roasted it was done in pans, as it still is in parts of Ethiopia and Yemen. The Turkish-style oval roaster has been used for hundreds of years and can produce a good roast. Popcorn roasters can yield very good results too. Modern home electric coffee roasters can be programmed to give you exact roasts for different beans and styles of coffee making.

DEGREE OF ROAST (BY COLOUR)

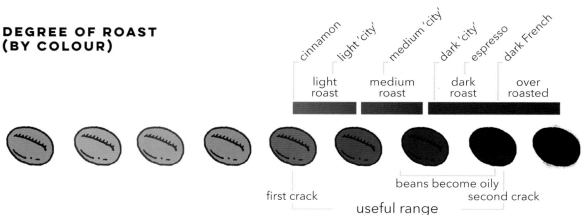

cinnamon · light 'city' · medium 'city' · dark 'city' · espresso · dark French

light roast · medium roast · dark roast · over roasted

first crack

beans become oily

second crack

useful range

PAN ROASTING

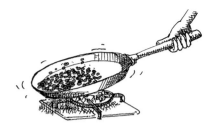

Place 100 g (3½ oz) of coffee in a heavy pan. Place the pan over a medium heat and keep the beans moving throughout the roast. This will keep the roast even, and avoid burning.

The colour of the beans slowly changes throughout the roast. You will hear a quiet crackling (the 'First Crack') as the beans start to brown. From this point it's a matter of choice how dark you wish to roast.

OVEN ROASTING

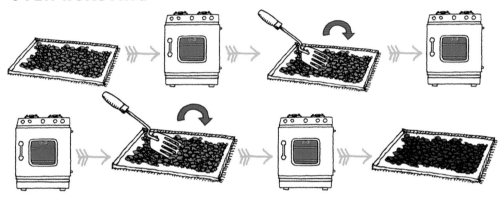

Place 100g (3½ oz) of beans in a single layer on a baking tray. Transfer it to an oven pre-heated to 180°C (350°F). Every 4 minutes take the beans out and turn them. Remember to take them out to cool when they're a shade lighter than the desired roast colour.

COOLING & STORAGE

To cool the beans and remove any chaff, put the beans into a metal colander and stir gently. The chaff should drop through the holes. Place the beans on a cold baking tray to finish cooling. Then put in a jar and store for 48 hours before use. For longer-term storage, put them in a ziplock bag, removing as much air as possible before placing the bag in the freezer.

GRINDING COFFEE

In Yemen and Ethiopia (where the coffee plant originates from) a pestle and mortar was used to grind coffee, and the results sieved to catch large particles. Coffee spread through the Muslim world, and it was probably the Turks who developed the first coffee grinding mills. By the mid-19th century, coffee grinders were common in homes, shops, and cafés. There have been great improvements in the last few years, which combined with the availability of really good coffee, have lifted the quality of the final drink.

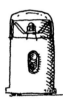

Blade

Conical burr

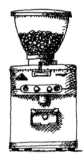

Flat plate burr

Blade 'grinders' are relatively cheap, but the grind is inconsistent and the particles vary widely in size. It may be extreme but to solve this problem some people sieve the ground coffee with different-sized meshes to get the particle size they desire. The blade grinder also creates heat, which is not ideal as it can affect flavour. When using a blade grinder, use a fixed amount, then adjust the timing so you can note the results and repeat them.

Burr grinders use abrasive, ridged surfaces to grind beans. A conical burr uses two cone-shaped grinding mechanisms lined with ridged surfaces. One burr is held in a fixed position slightly apart from the other burr which rotates. The position of the fixed burr can be adjusted to allow for different grind sizes. They are generally very good and produce useful grind sizes.

Flat plate grinders contain two large plates that face each other. Like the conical burr grinder, one plate remains stationary while the other moves. Each plate features teeth on the edges which crush and grind the beans. These machines also offer greater control of the distance between the plates and therefore the final grind size.

GRIND SIZE

Different brew methods (for example French press, Pour-over, etc.) work best with specific grind sizes as the latter affects the diffusion of the flavour and/or the movement of liquid through the process. While there is no absolutely correct size, conventions have developed over time, and are widely accepted as being a good starting point.

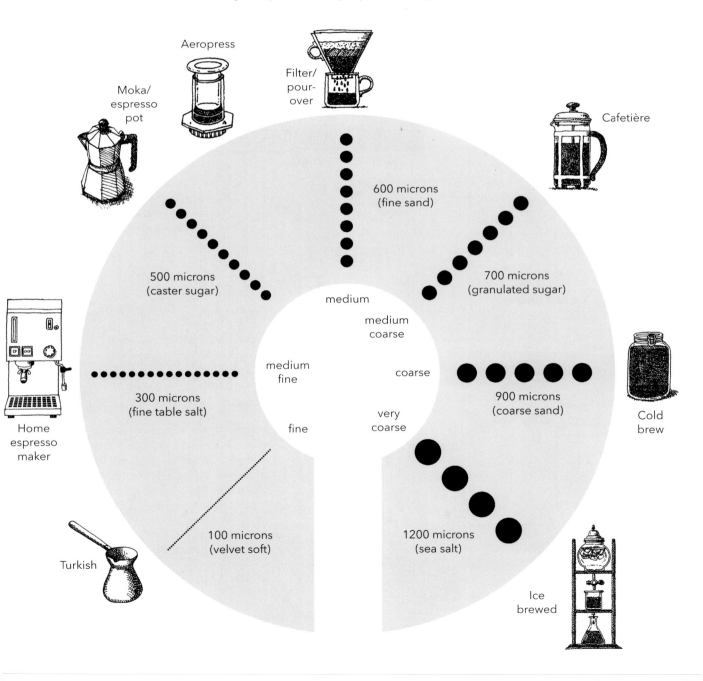

Moka/espresso pot

Aeropress

Filter/pour-over

Cafetière

600 microns (fine sand)

700 microns (granulated sugar)

500 microns (caster sugar)

medium

medium coarse

Home espresso maker

medium fine

coarse

900 microns (coarse sand)

Cold brew

300 microns (fine table salt)

fine

very coarse

100 microns (velvet soft)

1200 microns (sea salt)

Turkish

Ice brewed

FOAMING &
STEAMING MILK

with
an espresso
machine

Steaming and/or foaming the milk adds texture and some sweetness. Skimmed or semi-skimmed milk (below 2% fat) is much easier to foam, but with experience full-fat milk can be foamed and will add a richer quality to the coffee.

[1] After filling the water reservoir of the espresso maker, switching it on, and waiting for it to heat up and come to pressure, make sure the wand is clean and clear by carefully venting it into a safe container.

[2] Fill a jug with the milk. Aim for about half-full for foaming, but if you are just steaming it, you can add a little more.

[3] When you start to use the steam wand, make sure the end of the nozzle is below the surface of the milk, and open the steam tap slowly.

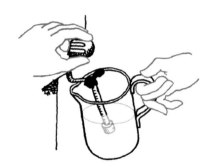

TEMPERATURE

Steaming or foaming take the temperature of the milk up to around 65–70°C (149–158°F), but no hotter because this will 'scald' the milk. Milk thermometers can be bought cheaply and are very useful, but there is a lag in the time between heating and the reading on the thermometer that you should be aware of. If you don't have a thermometer you can judge the temperature with your hand if you are careful. If the jug is too hot to hold, it's too hot…

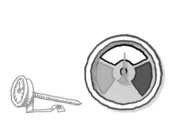

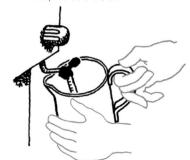

STEAMING

Place the nozzle about two-thirds of the way down into the milk, and turn on the steam with the nozzle in the milk to avoid splattering. Try to create a gentle whirlpool by rotating the nozzle and moving it up and down. The volume of the milk should only increase a little.

positioning the wand to create a whirlpool

FOAMING

Steam wands come with two different types of tip:

Standard Tip The tip is held very close to the surface so that as the steam is vented, air is drawn into a flow from the surface of the milk.

Easy Foaming Tip This tip has a hole to allow air in, which mixes with the steam and milk. It is held in the milk with the air hole above the surface.

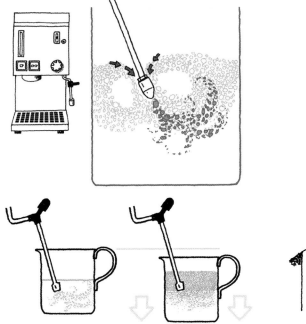

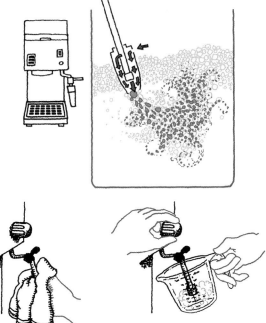

With either type of wand the jug should be slowly lowered as the foam level rises so the nozzle remains in the same position relative to the surface.

Immediately wipe the nozzle with a clean damp cloth to avoid milk 'baking on', and then run the steam for 5 seconds to clean out the end.

FOAMING & STEAMING MILK

without an espresso machine

You can use a stove-top frother to create foamed or steamed milk. These work well, but it is best to choose those with a holder for the lid because it allows you to hold the lid down properly and prevent burning yourself. Again it is best used with a thermometer.

FROTHING JUGS

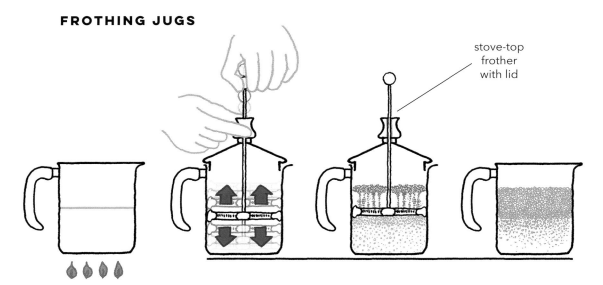

stove-top frother with lid

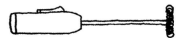

Half-fill the pot with milk and put over a moderate heat. When the milk has reached 65°C (149°F), take it off the heat and place on a solid surface. Froth until the milk volume fills three-quarters of the pot. Avoid pulling up too hard as it may bring milk up over the top of the pot.

BATTERY-POWERED FROTHERS

Battery-powered frothers require the milk to be pre-heated, and this can be done with a microwave. Fill a mug one-third full, and blast it for 60 seconds on full power. This should heat the milk to about 60°C (140°F). Put the mug on a firm surface. Place the end of the frother below the surface of the milk and froth until the mug is about half full.

MILK

Most cow's or goat's milk that you buy in shops has been processed by having the fat removed and then having some reintroduced (unless it is 'skimmed', and then it will only contain minute traces of fat). When the fat is reintroduced it is jetted into the milk at very high pressure to break up the fat into tiny droplets that will not separate out quickly. This is known as homogenization and does

affect the flavour. The other process that is commonly used on milk is pasteurization. The milk is rapidly heated to 72°C (161°F), held there for 15 seconds and then cooled rapidly to around 4°C (39°F) in order to kill bacteria. Where raw milk is available, it hasn't been treated with either of these processes or had the fat removed. It does taste good, but there is the risk of some bacterial contamination, and unlike pasteurized milk it will have a very short shelf life (a week compared with 2 weeks for pasteurized, but be guided by the 'use by date').

MILK ALTERNATIVES

Some people avoid animal milks for ethical reasons, while some cannot consume them due to lactose intolerance. In Europe approximately 10% of the population is lactose-intolerant, but in Africa, Asia, and Latin America, the percentage might be as high as 75%. As babies, almost everyone can consume milk because they produce an enzyme called lactase that breaks down lactose in the milk, but this ability 'switches off' (usually in early childhood) in those that become lactose-intolerant. Only a very small number of babies are actually born with lactose intolerance. The abdominal symptoms are not pleasant, but thankfully there are a lot of lactose-free alternative products that you can buy, or, you can make your own.

Nut milks

Soya milk

Oat milk

These are usually made by soaking the nuts, blending them with water and filtering through a specialized cloth or other fine filter.

Similar in process to nut milks but the milk must be boiled after straining and then cooled.

Blend 'rolled oats' in water, and then strain and squeeze through a specialized cloth.

All of these milks can be made with some sweetening and/or vanilla, but should not be kept for more than 2–3 days. Most will need to be shaken before use.

ESPRESSO-BASED DRINKS

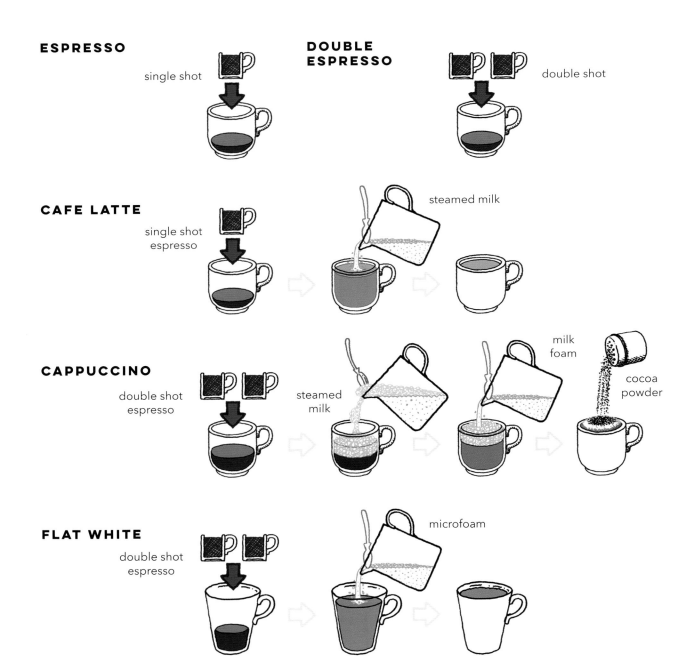

ESPRESSO

single shot

DOUBLE ESPRESSO

double shot

CAFE LATTE

single shot espresso

steamed milk

CAPPUCCINO

double shot espresso

steamed milk

milk foam

cocoa powder

FLAT WHITE

double shot espresso

microfoam

AMERICANO

double shot
espresso

hot water

CAFE MOCHA

double shot
espresso

hot
chocolate

steamed milk

MACCHIATO

double shot
espresso

milk foam

AFFOGATO

vanilla ice
cream

double shot
espresso

CAFETIÈRE/FRENCH PRESS

The modern cafetière/French press was actually designed by an Italian but the method was previously used in France. A stick with a cloth filter was used to push down the grounds in the coffee before it was served.

← Classic cafetière/
French press

How it works

The cafetière is one of the simplest methods for making a good cup of coffee and comprises little more than filtering after brewing. The grind size affects the flavour as the finer the grind the more quickly the bitter flavours are released from the coffee. Small particles may also pass through the filter mesh and 'bitter' the drink in the cup. Therefore it is better to use a coarser grind.

[1] Put 60–70 g (2½–3 oz) of coarsely ground coffee per litre (quart) of water in the cafetière, then add water 'just off the boil'.

[2] Wait 30 seconds before gently stirring until all the grounds are wetted.

[3] Place the top on the pot and wait for at least 5 minutes but no more than 8 minutes.

[4] Slowly press down the plunger and serve. The coffee is best drunk within 10 minutes.

CAFÉ AU LAIT

French-style 'café au lait' can be made with coffee from a cafetière/French press. It is often served for breakfast in a bowl alongside a croissant.

[1] Heat the milk in a pan until it starts to bubble at the edges. You can add a few drops of vanilla essence or heat the milk with a split vanilla pod (bean), if you like.

[2] Add the hot milk to the coffee in the ratio of 4 parts milk to one of coffee.

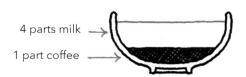

4 parts milk ⟶
1 part coffee ⟶

FILTER/POUR OVER COFFEE

German entrepreneur Melitta Bentz created a paper-based coffee filter in 1908. Initially she used blotting paper, but by 1930 her design was much as it is today. The advantage over a French press is that it removes bitterness by holding back very small particles.

Melitta coffee filter

TYPES OF FILTER DEVICE

Although there are a number of variations of the filter device, the main difference is in the filter papers, cloth, or metal cone used to filter the coffee. The rate at which the coffee escapes the 'funnel' may have some affect on taste; if it can only escape slowly then the brew will be prolonged and extract more flavour. This may lead to over-extracted, bitter coffee. This can be avoided by not using too fine a grind that will clog the filter.

Chemex coffee filter

FOLDING FILTER PAPERS

You can buy cone-shaped papers for these coffee makers but you can also use disc-shaped filter papers and fold them as shown here.

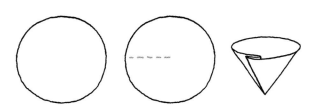

KETTLES & WATER

It is perfectly possible to make filter coffee with any device you can pour the heated water from, but there are now 'swan necked' kettles that allow the water to cool while travelling along the spout, and also allow greater control of the pouring.

[1] Place a filter in the holder and add the ground coffee.

[2] Slowly wet the coffee with water that has cooled for about 1 minute after boiling.

[3] Wait for 30 seconds for the coffee to absorb the water and swell (bloom).

[4] Slowly run a continuous stream of water from the kettle over the coffee, keeping the kettle moving.

[5] Wait for 30-60 seconds for the last of the drips to finish. The coffee is then ready to serve.

SYPHON COFFEE MAKER

Syphons have been available for around 100 years. It is the preferred method of some coffee experts and is possibly the visually most interesting.

How it works

The mechanism works by heating the water in a lower, sealed water chamber (the main jug) until it produces steam, creating pressure that pushes the remaining water up into another container (the 'tulip' bowl) where it mixes with ground coffee, and brews. The heat is then removed, and as the steam condenses in the lower chamber, it causes a drop in pressure that then pulls the brewed coffee back through a filter or small gap that separates out the grounds from the brewed coffee.

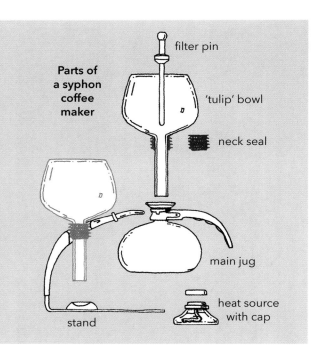

Parts of a syphon coffee maker

filter pin

'tulip' bowl

neck seal

main jug

heat source with cap

stand

[1] Fill the jug with boiling water. Make sure there is no water on the outside of the jug.

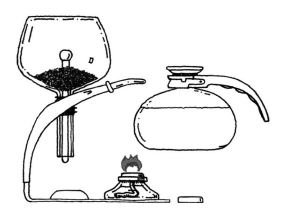

[2] Place the filter pin in the neck of the tulip bowl and add the ground coffee. Light the lamp and place the jug in the stand.

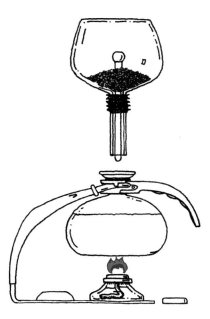

[3] Lower the tulip bowl into the neck of the jug and make sure it is fitted correctly. The rubber seal will fit quite tightly, which is essential for the process to work properly.

[4] As the water boils, the pressure will build, pushing the water up into the tulip bowl.

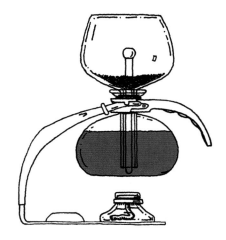

[5] When the water is in the tulip bowl, snuff out the lamp with its cap.

[6] The coffee will drip back into the jug, and once this is done, remove the tulip bowl and place it in its stand. The coffee is then ready to serve. If you wish to keep the coffee hot you can relight the lamp.

AEROPRESS COFFEE MAKER

The Aeropress has advantages over the filter in that it uses pressure to extract the coffee, and advantages over the French press in that it filters any fine particles from the brew.

STANDARD METHOD

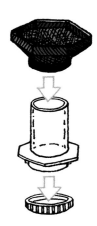

[1] Wet the filter and place in the cap.

[2] Fit the cap to the bottom of the barrel; attach the funnel at the top.

[3] Place the Aeropress over a cup; add the ground coffee at the top.

How it works

The Aeropress uses a hand-operated piston to push the brewed coffee down the barrel, and through a removable filter. It can make an espresso-strength brew (but doesn't produce a crema like an espresso machine), through to a more moderate filter-strength drink, dependant on the amount of coffee, brew time, coarseness of the grind, and the amount of water used.

Aeropress parts

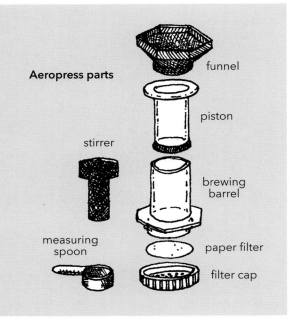

funnel

piston

stirrer

brewing barrel

measuring spoon

paper filter

filter cap

The Aeropress was designed by Alan Alder of the Aerobie Corporation in 2005. It's also extremely portable and now commonly used by many coffee professionals when they travel as well as at home. There are two different methods for brewing coffee in an Aeropress. The 'flip method' is slightly trickier but avoids coffee dripping through before it has brewed.

[4] Add water (just off the boil).

[5] Use the stirrer to stir for 10 seconds.

[6] Wait for 3 minutes, then press the piston down slowly.

FLIP METHOD

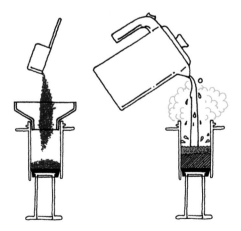

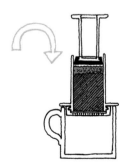
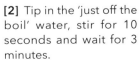

[1] Put the piston in the barrel, then flip the device upside-down. Put the funnel in; add the coffee.

[2] Tip in the 'just off the boil' water, stir for 10 seconds and wait for 3 minutes.

[3] Place a damp filter in the filter cap and screw securely onto the barrel.

[4] Flip the Aeropress over and place over a mug or cup. Then press down the barrel as usual.

STOVE-TOP/MOKA POT

The moka pot follows the same principle as the earliest espresso machines in that it uses steam pressure to force water through the coffee grounds. It will make espresso but won't make a crema in the same way that an espresso machine does.

[1] Water can be boiled in the pot from cold, but using boiling water from a kettle reduces the time the coffee grounds are exposed to heat and moisture and makes for better flavour. Fill the pot to just below the safety valve on the side.

[2] Fill the filter funnel with finely ground coffee until it is slightly heaped above the top edge, and then gently press down the coffee with a finger.

[3] Fit the filter funnel into the base. If you've used boiling water from a kettle, use a thick, dry cloth to hold the base pot.

How it works
The mechanism works by heating the water in a lower sealed water chamber until it produces steam, and then the pressure from increased volume (created by the steam) pushes the water up through the ground coffee, then through a filter (that holds back the coffee grounds), and finally into the upper chamber of the pot.

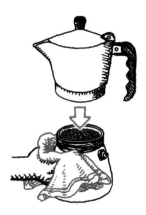

[4] Place the base of the pot on a work surface and then screw on the top of the jug.

[5] Place on the stove over a medium heat. You will hear gurgling and bubbling noises as the water is pushed through the coffee and enters the top chamber.

[6] Do not open the lid until the noise has stopped (there is a danger from boiling coffee), then turn off the heat and serve.

HISTORY AND MOKA POT VARIATIONS

The moka pot was patented in 1933 by Alfonso Bialetti, founder of the Bialetti Company, which produce an almost identical model to this day. Other companies have made variations but the Bialetti is the best known and most widely used. Variations include some pots that foam the milk with the coffee, another that is partially made of steel so it can be used on induction hobs, and others that use a cup to collect the coffee from a nozzle rather than collecting it in a chamber at the top of the pot.

Bialetti coffee pot

Stove-top pot with steam wand

Stainless steel stove-top pot

TURKISH-STYLE COFFEE

Turkish-style coffee is made from very finely ground coffee beans that are simmered in a traditional pot called an ibrik, which is made from copper or brass. You can, alternatively, use a small saucepan. Traditionally sugar and cardamom are added during brewing and the coffee is served with a glass of water. If you wish to sweeten the coffee during the making you should be very careful as the addition of the sugar will raise the boiling point of the liquid and can burn skin.

[1] Add 40 ml (7 tsp) of water for every cup, and sugar to taste into a Turkish coffee pot or saucepan.

[2] Heat the pot until it is very warm but do not allow it to boil.

[3] Add 15 g (½ oz) of coffee for every person.

[4] Wait until the coffee grounds start to sink and stir gently.

[5] Heat until foam builds up on the surface. Do not allow it to boil.

[6] Remove the foam from the top and scoop it into a bowl.

CARDAMOM

Turkish coffee is often served with cardamom. For each cup use one or two pods, crush them, discard the outer shells, then grind the seed finely, and add to the water at the start of the process.

[7] Heat the pot until the coffee starts to foam again.

[8] The coffee is now ready to serve. Pour into small cups and serve with a glass of cold water.

HISTORY & OTHER INFORMATION

Turkish coffee has been brewed in much the same way for the last 600 years, throughout much of the Middle East and Eastern Mediterranean. Similar brewing methods were used in Europe when coffee was first introduced there.

Hand-operated coffee grinders were developed to grind beans very finely. These are still available and function well for this type of grind. Very often, home burr grinders do not have a setting fine enough for Turkish-style coffee so check before purchasing one. Alternatively, buy a Turkish hand grinder, or buy a bag of pre-ground Turkish-style coffee if this interests you.

COLD BREW, DRIP & ICED COFFEE

One good reason to use a cold-brewed coffee (rather than a chilled hot brew) for cold drinks is that as hot coffee cools it becomes increasingly bitter. This doesn't happen when coffee is brewed cold. Cold-brewed coffee should be brewed with really good coffee as any failings in the quality of the coffee are obvious in the taste.

There are many cold-brew, drip, and iced-brew devices. These are convenient to use and can make good coffee. Some allow for the brewing and then release of the coffee into a collection container, while others allow for easy removal of the grounds.

Ice brewers are designed to slowly drip chilled water over the grounds, and the filtering and collection of the coffee. When making a cold or iced brew, bear in mind that the grind size and brewing time greatly affect the flavour.

TYPES OF DEVICE

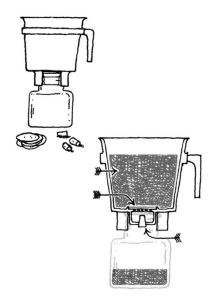

Toddy Brewer (cold brewer)

This is a container that you place ground coffee in, add water, allow to steep for 12–24 hours, and then remove a plug in the base of the brewer and drain the coffee off.

Hario Jug (infusion jug)

Brewed in a similar manner to the Toddy, but the coffee is contained in a central 'basket' filter that can be removed. The jug can be used to make infusions including teas.

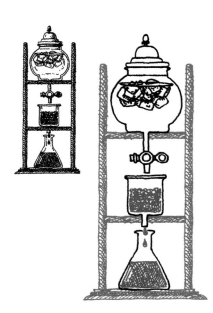

'Dutch' Ice Drip (ice drip brewer)

This system supplies chilled water to drip through a chamber containing coffee and then settle into a collection chamber beneath. The process takes 3–8 hours.

AD-HOC COLD BREW

If you don't have a device specifically for making cold-brew coffee, you can use other devices. Perhaps the most commonly used vessel is a large jar, which needs to be filtered after brewing. It is also possible to use a cafetière/French press or a jug and a coffee filter.

Glass Jar

Coffee Filter

Cafetière/French press

A large glass jar is perfectly adequate for making cold brew coffee. Add 14 g (½ oz) of coffee for every 100 ml (scant ½ cup) water. Then seal the jar, shake vigorously, and leave for 8 hours. The coffee should now be ready to serve but should be filtered first. This can be done with a paper filter or a clean cloth.

While not allowing a long brew time, it is possible to make cold brew by pouring cold/chilled water directly over the grounds. This makes a lighter, less bitter brew than most methods, and it can be drunk immediately.

With a cafetière you can mix cold water with the coffee, allow it to brew, and then use the plunger to filter the coffee before serving. The brew time can be anything from 10 minutes for a very light brew through to 8 hours.

SERVING

When the coffee has brewed, pour it into a jug and dilute to taste. And if you want to serve with ice, you can freeze some of the coffee in ice cubes so that the ice doesn't further dilute the coffee as it melts in the drink. Add milk, cream, and sugar as desired. The coffee can be stored in a fridge for several days.

D.I.Y. ICE COFFEE DRIPPER

Ice coffee drippers can be very expensive, but you can make your own using two 1-litre plastic soft drink bottles, a pin to make holes, a hole punch, and a sharp blade.

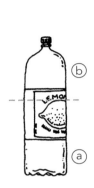

[1] Start by making the main 'coffee collector' (a) and the smaller 'top funnel' (b) by carefully cutting one of the plastic bottles two-thirds of the way up the bottle.

[2] Using a fine needle or pin, make a small hole through the cap. This can be enlarged if the flow is less than a few drips per minute when it is screwed on the funnel and filled with water.

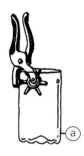

[3] Make some air holes close to the top of the 'coffee collector'. Without these the coffee cannot descend into the lower container if you form a seal with the large coffee holding funnel that fits into it.

[4] Cut the second bottle just over one-third of the way up the bottle to make the large holding funnel.

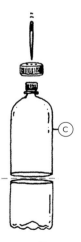

[5] Using the needle or pin, make holes in the second bottle cap (it doesn't need a restricted flow so make as many holes as you like).

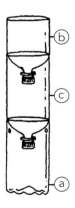

[6] The 'tower' can now be assembled, with the inverted bottle-top funnels fitting easily but tightly into the piece below.

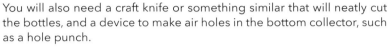
Materials
Use two large plastic soft drink bottles or any other container that will fit together as described, but it is important that the containers have lids that you can puncture with a sharp needle.

You will also need a craft knife or something similar that will neatly cut the bottles, and a device to make air holes in the bottom collector, such as a hole punch.

USING YOUR ICE DRIPPER

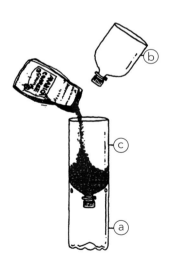

[1] Put 100 g (3½ oz) of coffee in the large funnel.

[2] Fix the smaller funnel in place with its cap, and then fill it with ice.

[3] Wait for 6–8 hours for the coffee to col,lect in the base and serve.

TEA

HISTORY

Tea has been found in tombs in China that are 1800 years old, but it was in the Han dynasty (618-906 AD) that is became widely drunk across China. During the latter part of this period tea travelled to Japan and started to be drunk there. The Dutch who were trading with China brought back tea for the first time to Europe in about 1606, and it became popular in Holland before spreading across Europe. By 1664, the British were starting to import tea, and it became very popular. Later the British managed to steal the plant from China and set up plantations in India. For a long period Britain had strong control over the international tea market and is still actively involved in the trade.

BIOLOGY

Green and black tea both come from the same plant, *Camellia sinensis*, that will grow in tropical and sub-tropical parts of the world, but originated in China and northern Burma. The plant will grow into a tree but for ease of harvesting it is pruned to the shape of a bush. Only the top leaves of mature plants are picked, and in season these regrow and can be harvested every week or two. Many of the high-quality tea plants are grown at high elevations (up to 1500 m/5000 ft above sea level), where they grow more slowly.

CHEMISTRY

Like coffee, tea contains caffeine as a method of self protection, and it accounts for 3% of a tea's dry weight. Green tea can contain twice as much caffeine as black tea (which is roasted). Much of the taste of tea is from polyphenols that include tannin. These give astringency and add to mouth feel. Various health claims are made for tea but few are scientifically proven. The time taken to drink tea (in most cases) probably gives some provable benefit.

BASIC TEA METHOD

Tea making varies around the world but in the West, a method has developed over the past few hundred years that is very common, and widely used with both single type and blended teas.

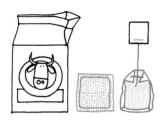

[1] Empty any previously boiled water away and then fill your kettle with an adequate amount of water for your tea making (however many cups plus enough to warm the teapot [step 2]).

[2] As soon as the kettle has fully boiled, tip about a cup full of water into the pot and gently swirl the water around the pot to warm it.

[3] Tip away this water because it will now be too cool to use to make tea.

[4] Add a teaspoon of tea or a teabag for each cup, plus one additional teaspoon or bag if you prefer your tea stronger.

[5] Add the water from the kettle. The temperature will have dropped a little after boiling but this is recommended by tea professionals.

[6] Leave the tea to brew for 3-5 minutes.

[7] Add milk to the cup before pouring the tea out - this will raise the temperature of the milk slowly as it is mixed with the tea and avoids 'scorching' the milk.

[8] Pour out the tea and serve.

[9] If you want to make tea in a mug with a teabag, it is worth warming the mug with water, emptying it, then adding the bag and fresh water. This will mean adding the milk to the hot tea so try to wait until the tea has cooled a little first.

BREWING

JAPANESE GREEN

Temperature: 82°C (180°F)

Brewing time: 2½-3 minutes

 1 teaspoon (level) to 175 ml (¾ cup) of water

BLACK

Temperature: 96°C (205°F)

Brewing time: 3-5 minutes

  1 teaspoon (heaped) to 175 ml (¾ cup) of water   Add milk or lemon, if desired

DARJEELING

Temperature: 85°C (185°F)

Brewing time: 3 minutes

 1 teaspoon (heaped) to 175 ml (¾ cup) of water   Add milk or lemon, if desired

EARL GREY

Temperature: 98°C (208°F)

Brewing time: 3-5 minutes

 1 teaspoon (heaped) to 175 ml (¾ cup) of water   Add milk or lemon, if desired

WHITE

Temperature: 85°C (185°F)

Brewing time: 1-3 minutes

 1 teaspoon (heaped) to 175 ml (¾ cup) of water

CHINESE GREEN

Temperature: 85°C (185°F)

Brewing time: 3 minutes

 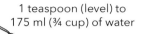

1 teaspoon (level) to 175 ml (¾ cup) of water

GUNPOWDER TEA

Temperature: 82°C (180°F)

Brewing time: 2-4 minutes

1 teaspoon (level) to 175 ml (¾ cup) of water

JASMINE

Temperature: 80°C (176°F)

Brewing time: 2-4 minutes

1 teaspoon (heaped) to 175 ml (¾ cup) of water

Add lemon, if desired

HERBAL TEAS

Temperature: 97°C (206°F)

Brewing time: 7-10 minutes

1-2 teaspoons (heaped) to 175 ml (¾ cup) of water

GREEN TEA

Japanese-style green tea has become increasingly popular in the West over the last few years. It just takes a little more effort than conventional black teas to prepare. In Japan, it is traditionally served in a 'chawan' (tea bowl), which are available to buy online.

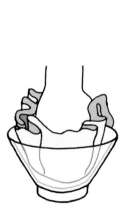

[1] As with other teas, boil a kettle of fresh water, and as soon as the kettle has boiled, fill the tea bowl to warm it.

[2] Empty the bowl and then dry it with a cloth.

[3] Sieve a teaspoonful of the green tea powder through a fine sieve into the warmed bowl.

There is a long and time-honoured history of tea-making in Japan and specific traditions and equipment have developed for every part of it. While each element enhances the tea to a very high level, it is possible to make green tea to a good standard. Perhaps the most necessary implement is a whisk. Traditional whisks can be found for sale online, but a small electric whisk can be used as well.

[4] Add water that has cooled to 82°C (180°F) from the kettle to the bowl, filling it about two-thirds full.

[5] Using a whisk, beat gently until the tea is frothed and mixed.

[6] Serve.

MINT TEA

In North Africa and the Middle East, fresh mint tea is very popular. There are variations of mint tea that just use fresh mint leaves, which is then sweetened with either honey or sugar (lemon is sometimes added, too), and then there is also a tea brewed with green tea leaves and mint leaves, as shown below.

To make a mint-only based tea, place a small bunch of mint leaves in a cup or glass, or torn leaves in a small sieve that is placed in the mouth of a glass. Just-boiled water is then poured over the mint leaves, and left to brew for a few minutes. Remove the leaves, sweeten to taste, and add lemon if desired.

[1] Add a teaspoon of loose green tea for each cup of tea you want into a teapot.

[2] Add about a cup of water from a just-boiled kettle.

[3] Allow the tea to brew for no more than 1 minute.

[4] Pour away the brewed tea from the pot (in this method this 'tea' is discarded, but in some methods it is used).

[5] Add a handful of mint leaves to the pot. Various mints can be used including spearmint leaves and peppermint leaves.

[6] Add more freshly boiled water to the pot and allow it to brew for 4–5 minutes.

[7] Serve in a glass or cup, sweeten with sugar or honey, and add lemon if desired.

CHAI TEA

In India, chai tea is a spiced milky tea that is usually sweetened. There are variants of chai around the world and it has become very popular in the West. The basic preparation process is simple. Spices commonly used in chai tea include ginger, cardamom, cloves, black pepper, cinnamon, star anise, fennel, and coriander seeds. The instructions below are for a masala chai tea.

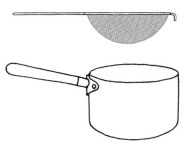

[1] Add 2 thin slices of fresh ginger, a short piece of cinnamon stick, 6 cardamom pods, 8 cloves, and ½ star anise to a saucepan and simmer for 5 minutes.

[2] Turn off the heat and allow the mixture to steep for 10 minutes, then sieve the liquid to remove the spices.

[3] Add a teaspoon of tea along with 500 ml (2 cups) of milk, and return to the heat. Bring to a simmer, strain, and then serve. Sweeten as desired.

COLD BREW TEA

Cold brew teas can have a very different flavour profile from those brewed hot. This is because the diffusion of the chemical compounds in the tea into the water will happen more slowly and at different rates when the water is colder. You can use a lot of the same equipment that you use for making cold-brew coffee (see page 126) because the process is very similar. The brewing times vary from method to method.

SUN TEA

In many parts of the USA there is a tradition of making 'Sun Tea'. This is brewing tea in a glass container that is warmed by sunlight. While it is thought by some that the light is largely responsible for the brewing flavour, it is in fact just the warmth that affects the brewing. To avoid bacterial growth, it is best to transfer the tea to the refrigerator when it has reached the strength you desire (after 3-5 hours in the sun). It will keep in the fridge for 2 days.

[1] Using either boiled water that has been allowed to cool (direct from the tap, chlorine may taint the taste), filtered water, or still bottled water, fill a jar or other container.

[2] Add 1½ teaspoons or one teabag per cup of water and place the container in the sunlight for 3-5 hours. Add herbs to the 'brew' if you wish.

[3] Serve, with sugar and lemon if desired.

HOT CHOCOLATE & COCOA

Chocolate is produced from cocoa beans, the dried seed of the cacao tree, which is native to the Americas. Chocolate has a history that may go back 7,000 years. and it was widely used in cooking and as a drink. The Aztecs introduced it to the Spanish, who brought it back to Europe. In Mexico, the beans were traditionally ground up, and then heated with water, honey, chilli, and vanilla. In Europe the spicing changed and it was mixed with milk.

AZTEC-STYLE CHOCOLATE

Although this is not the actual method the Aztecs used, it does replicate the flavour fairly closely. If you wish to take this further you can add ground maize.

Ingredients
500 ml (2 cups) water
75 g (2½ oz) 100% dark (bittersweet)
  chocolate (a Mexican brand if you can)
a vanilla pod (bean)
1 dried Guajilllo chilli
honey, to taste

[1] Place all the ingredients (except the honey) in a saucepan and heat gently while whisking continuously for 10 minutes. Sieve and serve with honey to taste.

FRENCH-STYLE HOT CHOCOLATE

When drinking chocolate arrived in Paris, it became very popular. It was made with Mexican-style hand-grinding stones which would have produced quite a coarse chocolate by modern standards, but the ingredients were very similar to those that are still used today.

Ingredients
500 ml (2 cups) whole milk
125 g (4½ oz) 70% (or higher) dark
  (bittersweet) chocolate
a small pinch of salt
sugar, to taste

[1] Stir the milk, chocolate, and salt over a gentle heat until all the chocolate is integrated with the milk and the mix thickens a little. Don't let it boil. Then serve and sweeten to taste.

COCOA

Cocoa powder was first produced when the Dutch developed a technique to remove the cocoa butter from the ground beans, leaving a solid with less fat that could be powdered. Later, the Dutch developed a method to reduce the acidity of the cocoa, and this is what is known as 'Dutch Process Cocoa'. It is lighter in colour than natural cocoa and is the basis for most modern chocolate.

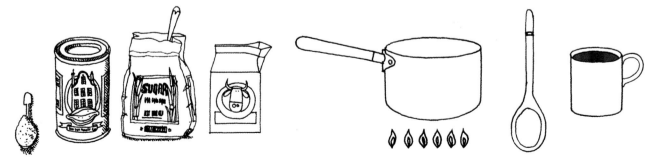

[1] To make hot cocoa, mix 2 tablespoons of cocoa with 1 tablespoon of sugar. When combined keep stirring as you add 250 ml (1 cup) of milk. Tip into a saucepan and stir as you heat until it is close to boiling. Serve.

JUICING

There are many different types of juicer available today and not all of them are suitable for all tasks. Check reviews online as juicers can vary greatly in usability and quality.

CITRUS JUICERS

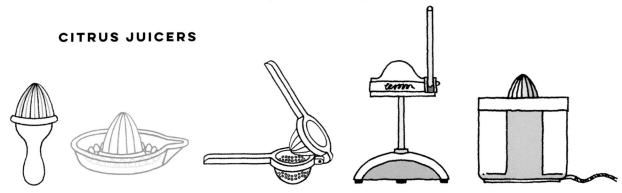

The simplest juicers are probably those for citrus. These use pressure and rotation to remove the juice from the flesh. You can use other types of juicer for citrus but it may involve the removal of the peel. If you use more than a little citrus for juicing, you should consider an electric or lever machine. For limes a 'lime' or 'citrus squeezer' works well and are commonly used in commercial bars.

ROTARY MILL JUICERS

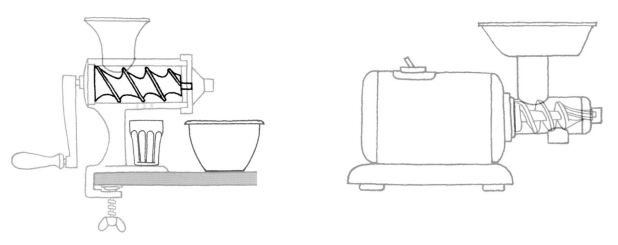

Rotary mill juicers are good for harder fruit and vegetables, as well as herbs and wheat grass. They are not particularly fast so are more suitable for lower volumes of juice.

CENTRIFUGAL JUICERS

Centrifugal juicers are good as a general juicer and if the inlet tube is large enough for whole fruit, it requires little preparation of the fruit/vegetables. These machines finely grate, and then spin the vegetable matter so the juice separates and runs out to be collected. The pulp also collects in a waste collector. These machines can take a lot of cleaning, though.

HYDRAULIC JUICERS

Hydraulic juicers use a powered press to extract the juice but to do this, the fruit or vegetables need to be ground quite small before they are pressed. These machines therefore sometimes come with a grinder for preparation.

SMOOTHIES & SHAKES

SHAKES

Milkshakes were originally made by hand in the late 19th century in the United States and often contained alcohol. By the end of the century non-alcoholic shakes became popular and were often served in drugstores. In 1911, the Hamilton Beach Company invented a drinks mixer, and an electric version was developed in 1922. These became very popular. 'Straws' made from dried natural grasses have been used for thousands of years, but in the 1880s a waxed paper straw was invented. These were narrow and people tended to use two at the same time. Then, in 1937, American inventor Joseph Friedman invented a straw that was not only wider, but also capable of being bent. Though most modern straws are plastic they follow the design of the original 1937 Friedman straw.

Early shakes were a mix of ingredients that might include milk, fruit syrups, ice cream, and malt powder.

A typical recipe might include: 2 large dessertspoons of ice cream or yogurt, 1 banana, 400 ml (1¾ cups) of milk (dairy, soya, or nut), and a spoonful of malt drink powder (such as Ovaltine). Put all ingredients into the machine and blend until smooth. Serve.

SMOOTHIES

As electric blenders became more powerful, they became capable of blending tougher materials such as fibrous vegetables and even nuts. This allowed a far wider range of flavours to be used and rather than being called shakes, they started to be called smoothies because of their texture. This also meant that is was possible to produce savoury (rather than sweet) drinks.

  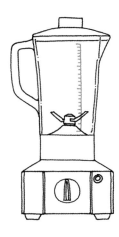

[1] Select the combination of ingredients you wish to use. If you have too much for a single session and want to make further shakes at a later time, it is worth 'bagging' groups of ingredients so you can just go to a single bag for the ingredients you need.

[2] Cut any large fruit or vegetables into pieces or strips (as whole fruit will often not blend). Place in the blender and process.

[3] If the mix doesn't combine, it may be because it is too dry, in which case add a little liquid. This can be water, fruit or vegetable juice, or coconut milk. If you want to have a chilled drink you can also add ice but it's best to freeze juice in a cube tray, as it won't dilute the flavour of the smoothie.

SODA & CARBONATION

In the process of carbonation, carbon dioxide (CO_2) is dissolved in a liquid so that it forms bubbles in the drink. Nitrogen or nitrous oxide is also used to add bubbles to liquids and foams but this is unusual in the home apart from some canned beers, which use a mix of CO_2 and nitrogen to give a very smooth, bubbly texture. Nitrous oxide is also used to 'whip' cream under pressure.

Carbonated water supplied in bottles usually has gas added to it at the bottling plant, although a very small number of spring waters are naturally carbonated. You can carbonate your own water with a soda syphon or a soda stream-type device. While it is possible to carbonate flavoured drinks at home, any flavourings will need to be added afterwards. Otherwise, the CO_2 can foam out very quickly and lose its fizz. CO_2 is also vastly more soluble in cold water than warm water, so keep water cold when carbonating it and chill the container before using it so that the bubbles last longer.

SODA SYPHON

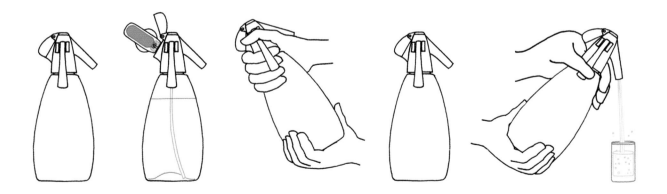

Remove the top and after rinsing it out, fill with cold water. You can add mineral salts if you like, such as Epsom salts, which can make the water more like a commercial soda water in taste. Screw on the top, attach a CO_2 cartridge and allow it to discharge. Shake the syphon as the gas is discharging. Allow to settle in a refrigerator.

SODASTREAM™

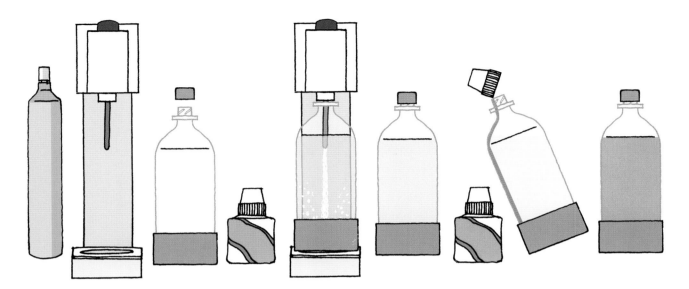

Sodastream™ is a carbonation system for use at home. CO_2 (supplied in exchangeable bottles) is jetted into reusable bottles that the user adds water to. Once the gas has caused the escape valve to 'burp' a couple of times, the user slowly unscrews the bottle from the stand and screws on a bottle cap. It is then best to chill the bottle and let it settle before adding a flavour concentrate if you wish to make a flavoured soda.

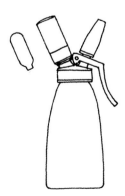

CREAM WHIPPERS

Pressurized cream whippers can be used for carbonation but also for flavour extraction. By placing a liquid and a flavoured herb, spice, etc., in the whipper and pressurizing and releasing the pressure rapidly, the liquid is forced into the herb or spice. Then when the pressure is released rapidly, the flavour comes out with the liquid's movement.

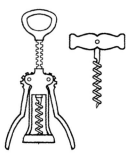

WINE

There are many types of corkscrew, but perhaps the most useful and popular are the basic corkscrew, the 'waiter's friend', and the twin lever.

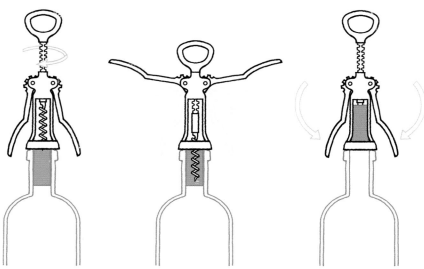

The lever corkscrew is simple to operate once you know that the levers start facing downwards, then rise as the screw is wound into the cork. Once the arms are up, gently use both hands to push the levers down, releasing the cork.

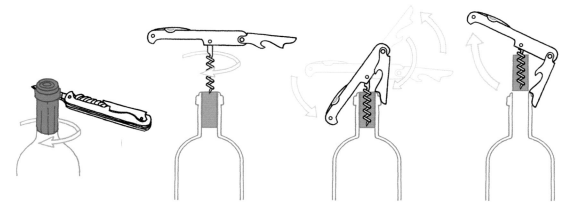

The 'waiter's friend' is useful in that it also has a knife to remove the foil from the bottle neck, and usually also has a beer bottle opener built in. The body acts as a handle when winding the corkscrew in, and as a lever when lifting out the cork from the bottle neck.

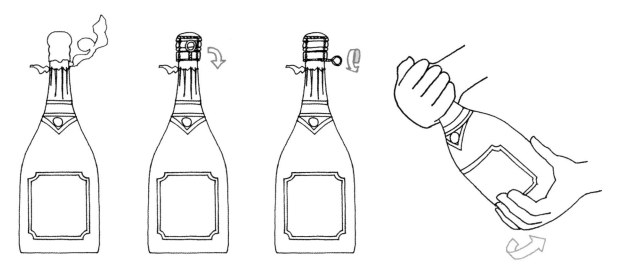

Champange is often opened with a gushing and loss of liquid, but with a little care you can open the bottle and preserve the liquid and retain almost all the bubbles. Remove the foil over the wire-caged cork, then lower the twisted wire loop 90 degrees and rotate it with six half turns and remove the wire. Holding the cork tightly in one hand, rotate the base of the bottle and slowly allow the cork to rise from the neck of the bottle. If you do this correctly it will release with a gentle hiss.

Once a bottle of wine is open it will oxidize and degrade over time and may also turn to vinegar. In the short term, wine can be stored in its bottle, but it is best to cover the neck with a seal such as clingfilm (plastic wrap). It is commonly believed that a spoon in the neck of a Champagne bottle will preserve the bubbles. IT DOES NOT. If you want to preserve bubbles, cover the neck with clingfilm (plastic wrap) and store cold in a fridge (CO_2 is more soluble in a cold liquid).

Wine will taste quite different when oxygenated and this is why some wines are traditionally decanted before drinking. An extreme version of this is to blend the wine in a blender. It is really surprising how different it tastes, and how many eyebrows it raises.

COCKTAILS

Cocktail equipment has developed over the last 100 years or so and includes three basic types of shaker, along with strainers, jiggers, and the muddler.

Boston Shaker A two-piece shaker used in bars as they are fast and hold larger volumes than other shakers. Ingredients and ice are put in the larger cup and the other cup is pushed tight in to make a seal. It is used with a strainer.

The Cobbler is a three-piece shaker and is the one most commonly found in homes. It has a built-in strainer and is a sensible option for those who don't have to make a large number of cocktails.

The 'French' or 'Parisian' is a two-piece shaker that is said to be easier to split after shaking than either of the others, but it is smaller than the Boston and doesn't have a strainer, so is not as popular.

If you don't have a 'cobbler' there will be times when you need a strainer. There are two basic types:

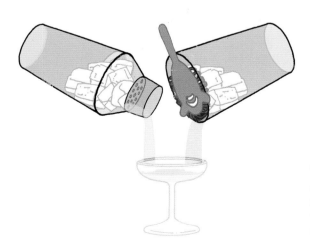  

The Hawthorne strainer has a wound spring to help strain and the Julep strainer looks like a perforated spoon. The Hawthorne fits the Boston shaker well, and the Julep works better with a stirring glass. You can get away with just owning one of them.

SHAKING & STIRRING

To properly shake a cocktail, shake for 10–15 seconds and ensure that you shake along the length/height of the shaker.

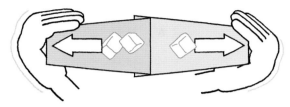

To stir a drink, take a barspoon between your thumb and first two fingers, allow the spoon to touch the bottom of the glass and stir for 30–60 seconds.

The difference between stirring and shaking is that shaking will introduce small bubbles and some texture to the cocktail, while stirring will not disturb the drink in this way. Drinks that largely comprise spirits tend to be stirred, as do any drink that has a carbonated element to it.

To stir a cocktail, pre-chill both the stirring glass and the serving glass with ice and water for 5 minutes, or in a freezer. Tip away any water, add the ingredients over the ice. Insert the spoon into the glass all the way to the bottom and stir gently for 60 seconds. Strain into the serving glass.

Muddling is the gentle grinding of ingredients for cocktails. Smooth-ended muddling sticks are good for herbs, and toothed sticks work for fruit but may be too harsh for herbs. Place herbs, sugar, fruit, etc., in the base of the glass and gently press and rotate the stick. The bitterness in mints and other herbs is in the stems and thicker structure of the herbs, so to avoid adding bitterness, try not to break, their structure.

Cocktail measures are known as jiggers. While traditional metal measures are good for single or double measures, a measure with small divisions is more useful. Many recipes are finely balanced for taste and can be followed more easily if you can measure fine quantities.

TYPES OF DRINKING GLASS

There are a huge variety of drinking glass and it would be impossible to list them all, but below are some of the more common glasses used for serving cocktails and other types of alcoholic drinks. Beyond the basic function of holding the drink, many of the glasses have other functions in their design such as insulating the drink, and retaining aroma and carbonation. For many years lead was used in the production of glasses, particularly for cut crystal, but this has become less common.

WINE GLASSES

Nearly all common wine glasses have a bowl, stem, and foot. If held by the stem it will avoid heat transferring from the hand to the wine contained in the glass. This is seen as important with white, or sparkling wines (such as Champagne). The lip of the bowl is usually narrower than the widest part of the bowl, and this may help to hold the aroma so when a drink is taken the scent of the wine becomes part of the experience. Using a glass tumbler to drink wine has been common in informal situations for a long time.

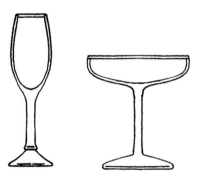

Red and white wine glasses are similar but the bowl of the white wine glass is usually a little slimmer.

Champange 'flutes' are tall and narrow to preserve the carboantion (bubbles), by having the minimum surface area. Wider coupe-style glasses that are sometimes used will allow the drink to go 'flat' very quickly'.

COCKTAIL GLASSES

Cocktails glasses can be roughly divided into those with stems, and those without. Their usage can usually be determined by how the drink is prepared. If the drink is stirred or shaken over ice, and then strained, then a stemmed glass is used to preserve its temperature, but if the drink poured over ice, or 'built' in the glass, it is usually served in a stemless glass.

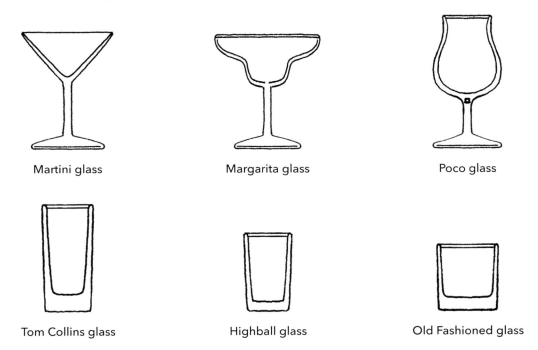

Martini glass   Margarita glass   Poco glass

Tom Collins glass   Highball glass   Old Fashioned glass

SPIRIT GLASSES

Spirit glasses are often chosen to enhance the experience of drink the particular spirit, but in the case of shot and shooter glasses it is perhaps to aid the rapid despatch of a drink. Good-quality spirits, such as malt whiskeys and Cognac, are often drunk slowly to appreciate the flavour, and the glasses they are served in are designed to add the enjoyment.

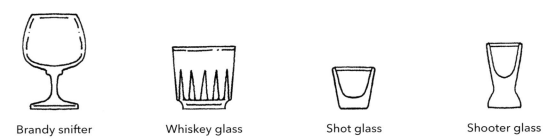

Brandy snifter   Whiskey glass   Shot glass   Shooter glass

BELLINI

Ingredients and ratio of parts: 5 fresh peach juice, 10 Prosecco
Technique: Stir
Glass: Champagne

BLACK RUSSIAN

Ingredients and ratio of parts: 2 coffee liqueur, 5 vodka, ice
Technique: Stir
Glass: Old-fashioned

BLOODY MARY

Ingredients and ratio of parts: 1.5 lemon juice, 2 dashes each of celery salt, pepper, Worcestershire sauce, Tabasco, 9 tomato juice, 4.5 vodka, ice
Technique: Stir
Glass: Highball

CUBA LIBRE

Ingredients and ratio of parts: 1 fresh lime juice, 5 white rum, 12 cola, ice
Technique: Build
Glass: Highball

CAIPIRINHA

Ingredients: 2 teaspoons sugar, half a fresh lime (muddled), 2 oz Cachaça, ice
Technique: Stir
Glass: Old-fashioned

COSMOPOLITAN

Ingredients and ratio of parts: 1.5 lime juice, 1.5 cointreau, 3 cranberry juice, 4 citron vodka, ice
Technique: Shake and strain
Glass: Cocktail

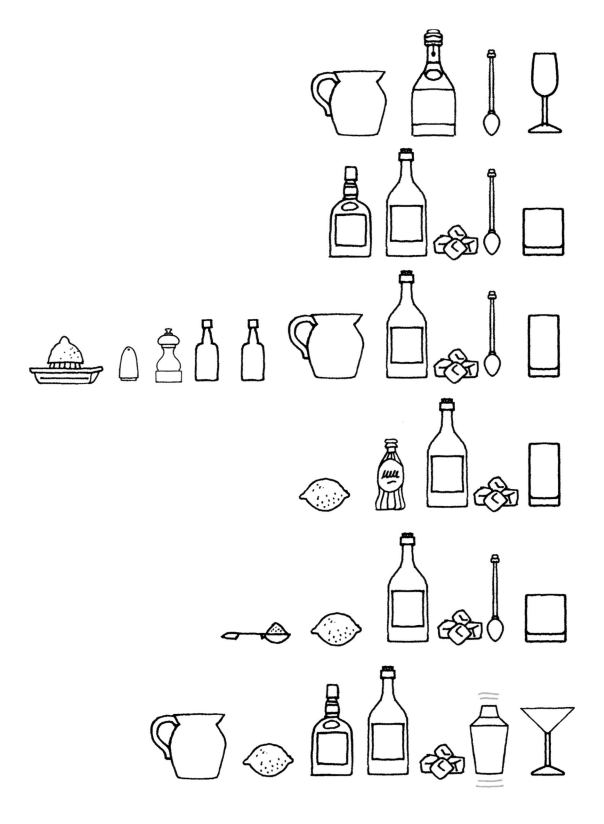

DAIQUIRI

Ingredients and ratio of parts: 1.5 simple syrup, 2.5 fresh lime juice, 4.5 white rum, ice
Technique: Shake and strain
Glass: Cocktail

DRY MARTINI

Ingredients and ratio of parts: 1 dry vermouth, 6 gin
Technique: Stir and strain, then garnish with a lemon twist or an olive
Glass: Martini

GIN FIZZ

Ingredients and ratio of parts: 8 soda water, 1 sugar syrup, 3 fresh lemon juice, 4.5 gin, ice
Technique: Build
Glass: Highball

JOHN COLLINS

Ingredients and ratio of parts: dash of angostura bitters, 1.5 sugar syrup, 3 fresh lemon juice, 4.5 gin, 6 soda water, ice
Technique: Stir
Glass: Collins glass

LONG ISLAND ICED TEA

Ingredients and ratio of parts: dash of cola, 1.5 tequila, 1.5 vodka, 1.5 white rum, 1.5 triple sec, 1.5 gin, 2.5 fresh lemon juice, 3 gomme syrup, ice
Technique: Stir
Glass: Highball

MAI-TAI

Ingredients and ratio of parts: 1 fresh lime juice, 1.5 orgeat syrup, 1.5 orange curaçao, 2 dark rum, 4 white rum, ice
Technique: Shake
Glass: Highball

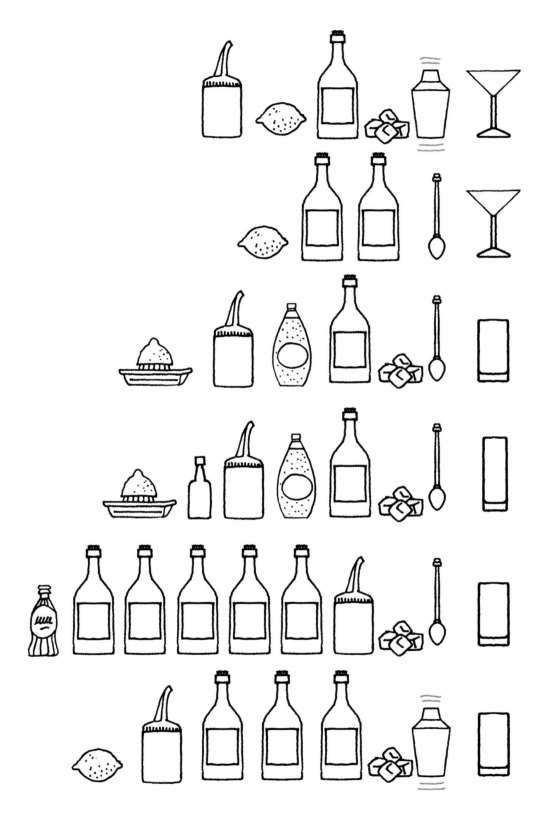

MANHATTAN

Ingredients and ratio of parts: 2 red vermouth, 5 rye whisky, dash of angostura bitters
Technique: Shake and strain
Glass: Cocktail

MARGARITA

Ingredients and ratio of parts: 1.5 fresh lime juice, 2 cointreau, 3.5 tequila
Technique: Shake and strain into a salt-rimmed glass
Glass: Margarita

MIMOSA

Ingredients and ratio of parts: 3 fresh orange juice, 3 Champagne
Technique: Stir
Glass: Champagne

MOJITO

Ingredients and ratio of parts: 2 teaspoons white sugar, 3 fresh lime juice, splash soda water, 4 white rum, 6 sprigs of fresh mint (muddled)
Technique: Stir
Glass: Collins

MOSCOW MULE

Ingredients and ratio of parts: 0.5 fresh lime juice, 4.5 vodka, 12 ginger beer
Technique: Pour
Glass: Copper mug

NEGRONI

Ingredients and ratio of parts: 3 red vermouth, 3 campari, 3 gin
Technique: Stir
Glass: Old-fashioned

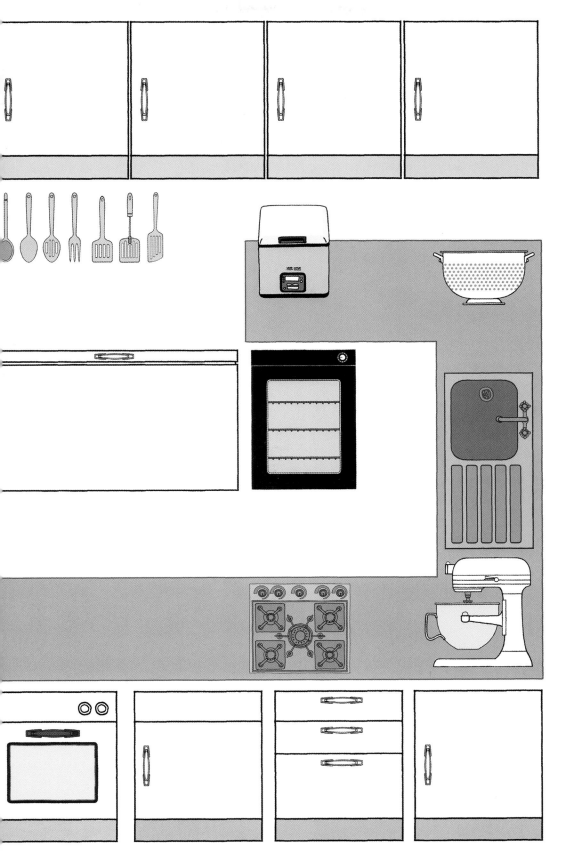

KITCHENS

KITCHENS

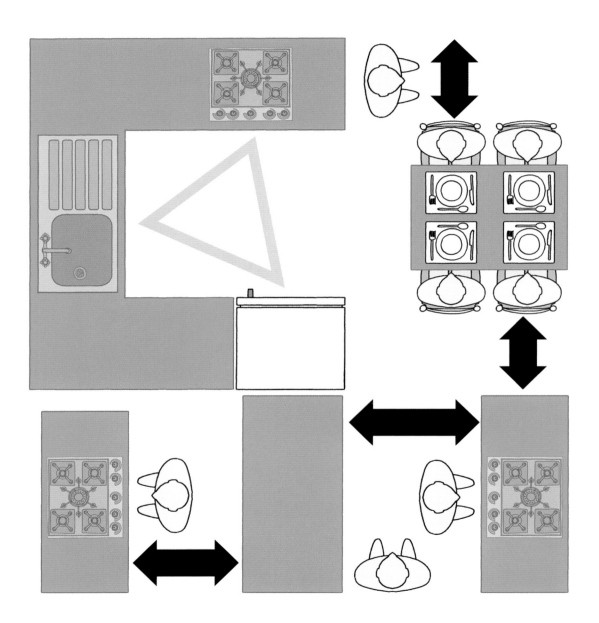

LAYOUT & USE

The kitchen is one of the only rooms in the house that is a workplace, and as such the way it works ergonomically will affect whoever's using it. Even small alterations can, over time, avoid annoyance, time wasting, and inconvenience, and make it a more enjoyable place. All layouts will be a compromise to some extent but just considering the factors that are affected by layout when drawing up plans for a kitchen will be beneficial.

While the following section tries to address some of the issues in kitchen design, there are complete books on the subject and even academics who study it.

KITCHEN WORK TRIANGLE

During the early part of the 20th century, industries developed methods for measuring the efficiency with which jobs were done. These were known as 'Time & Motion Studies'. In the 1940s, kitchen use was studied and theories of how to design kitchen layout developed from this. What was proposed was that the kitchen should be organized around the fridge, sink, and cooker, and that these should be placed in a manner that they were close enough to reach easily, but should give enough space around each of the 3 'corners' to be able to carry out any task that needed to be done there. While kitchens cannot always accommodate strict rules, the idea is worth considering.

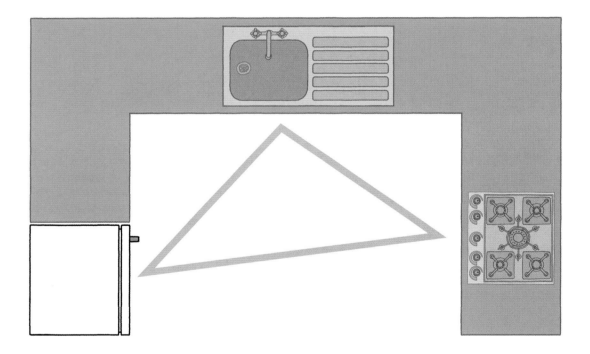

Although the kitchen work triangle was developed in a time before many modern appliances were invented or became popular, most work in the kitchen is still largely based around the triangle. The rules that were originally developed state that:

[1] Each point of the triangle should be between 1.2 and 2.7 m (4 and 9 ft) apart.
[2] The total of all the sides of the triangle should be 4–7.9 m (13–26 ft).
[3] No object should intrude into the triangle by more than 30 cm (12 inches).
[4] The triangle shouldn't be a general walkway for those not using the kitchen.
[5] No full-height object should be fixed between any of the points of the triangle.

SPACE

If possible, it is good practice to place units and kitchen furniture at distances apart that allow for free movement while working. This, of course, can also be a matter of safety in a kitchen when knives or hot items are present.

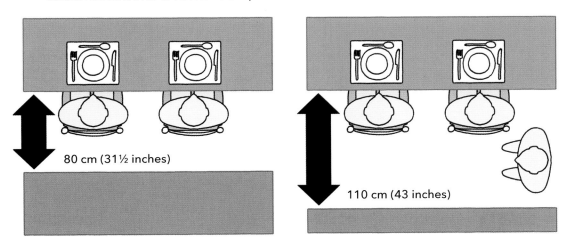

Where people are seated to eat at a table or bar, the distance between the surface they are eating at and any fixed obstruction such as a wall or units should be at least 80 cm (where there is no need to pass behind them), and 110 cm when it is necessary to maintain access.

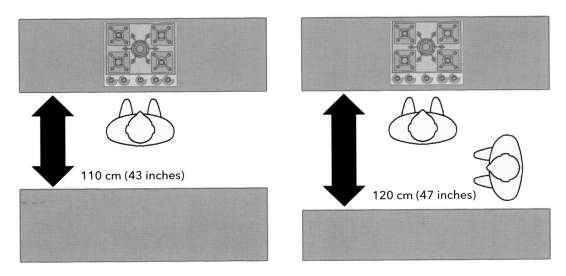

The distance between work surfaces are dependant on how many people are working in the kitchen. It is recommended that a single person needs 110 cm (43 inches) separation between the surfaces, whereas two people working require at least 120 cm (47 inches).

WORK SURFACES

There are many variations of work surface, each with different qualities, advantages and disadvantages. Cost is often the first consideration when choosing one, but there are other factors that should be considered.

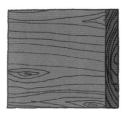

Single piece

This is made from a single piece and is often very beautiful but lacks stability and can warp. The wood used must be very carefully selected as some woods are unsuitable for work surfaces and can even be poisonous. You can seal the surface with oils or waxes.

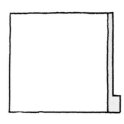

Joined

Joined blocks of wood used to make up a continuous surface are usually very stable as the joining largely removes the problem of warping. These surfaces are usually oiled or waxed but can be lacquered to preserve them.

End grain

Joined sections of end grain can be used to make a surface in a similar style to a butcher's block. Advantages are that the fibres are fairly resistant to cut marks, and also that many of the woods used have natural antiseptic properties. They can also be oiled or waxed.

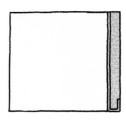

Laminates

There are many laminate work surfaces constructed over cores of wood chip or other material. These can be cheap or expensive, are practical for most kitchens, as well as being available in many designs. They are also easy to clean, and resistant to moderate heat. Some also have antiseptic qualities.

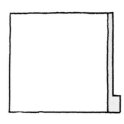

Polymer

These are usually a mix of a synthetic resin and a mineral dust, and are exceptionally hard wearing but expensive. As a result, they are often used in high-end kitchens. They are usually stain-resistant and can be cleaned with many chemical cleaners that would damage other surfaces.

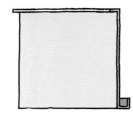

Stainless steel

Stainless steel is used in most commercial kitchens and has many advantages, as it is very tough, easily cleaned, and resistant to many heat sources. However, it does feel cold to work on, and is relatively difficult and expensive to custom-fit.

Quartz

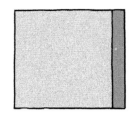

Granite

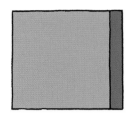

Slate

Quartz is a mineral but many 'quartz' work surfaces are in fact a mixture of quartz and a resin. This is often available in a range of marble and stone-effect finishes as well as some that are strongly coloured. They are often stain-resistant, unaffected by many chemicals, and tolerant of reasonable levels of heat.

Granite is extremely hard and is heat- and stain-resistant, but it is expensive because it is difficult to cut and join. Its colour is limited to its naturally occurring range but will not fade or discolour.

Slate is very limited in colour, cheaper than granite, resistant to heat, largely impervious to liquids, but it can be brittle on the edges so it is often recommended that the edges and corners are rounded off.

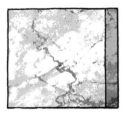

Marble

Concrete

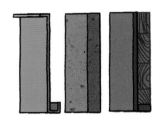

Other materials

Marble can be cheaper than quartz or granite but can stain as it is often quite porous. It can be sealed and polished but this can be expensive, and if the surface is damaged it will incur further costs. It is also not as hard as many other stone surfaces and can be damaged by a knife. If you choose marble there are quite a range of options and some are better than others. It's worth checking online for reviews.

Concrete can be plain or have colour, texture, or grain added. Generally it is expensive and must be sealed. Once sealed it makes a durable surface but may need resealing every few years. Very often a template is made for the surface and the concreate is cast offsite, but in some cases the concrete surface is cast in situ.

There are many other materials used for kitchen work surfaces including:

Copper is expensive, beautiful, and antibacterial but high-maintenance.

Resin can be plain or contain anything from broken glass to small toys, and lighting.

Tiles are hard wearing but problematic as joints can harbour dirt and bacteria unless treated.

WORK SURFACE POSITION

SURFACE HEIGHT

There is a standard height for kitchen work surfaces when you buy base units. This is 91cm (36 inches)to the top of the unit, and then the worktop surfaces are usually between 3–6 cm (1¼–2½ inches) deep dependant on the material. Dining and kitchen tables are often lower at approximately 74–80 cm (30–31½ inches). Some units have adjustable legs that can alter the height, but these are usually used to level the surface rather than add height or lower the whole unit. If you find the height of the work surface uncomfortable, it is possible to calculate the optimum height for yourself by measuring the distance from your fist to the floor. With cookers you know if it is too high if you have to raise your hand above your elbow as you cook.

UNIT & SURFACE DEPTH

Most work surfaces are supplied at a depth of 60 cm (23½ inches), which is the same as most base units and cupboards. When the work surface is placed on top of the units, the top height will vary according to the thickness of the surface, and this can throw the surface out of alignment with the top surface of stoves and other units. This is when the appliance height can be altered using adjustable legs to make sure that everything is level.

If base units are 60-cm (23½-inches) deep, it will be necessary to run the pipes under the units and up to the taps, or to drill through the sides of the cupboards to allow the passage of pipes. Some work surfaces are deeper, allowing you to bring the base units forward so the pipework can run behind them.

The cut-out at the bottom allows your feet to tuck slightly under the unit. If you don't have this cutout, it is difficult to balance close or work comfortably.

AMOUNT OF SURFACE NEEDED

The complexity and style of your cookery will influence how much space you need in the kitchen, but a rough guide for working is to have enough (as listed below) around the sink, cooker, and fridge to allow for preparation and to move ingredients and pans about as you work.

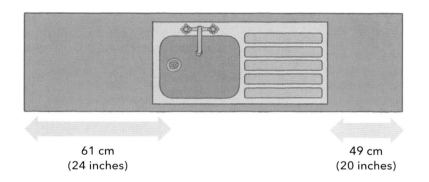

61 cm
(24 inches)

49 cm
(20 inches)

SINK

The sink should have at least 61 cm (24 inches) of work surface on one side and 49 cm (20 inches) on the other. The 61 cm (24 inches) section is the best area to use a chopping board.

FRIDGE FREEZER

On the door side of the fridge there should be a minimum of 38 cm (15 inches). If this not possible, then a counter with space should be close by.

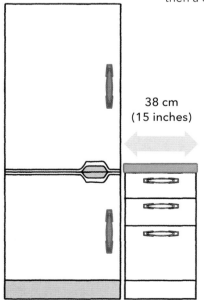

38 cm
(15 inches)

COOKER HOB

A cooking hob should have at least 38 cm (15 inches) on one side and 30 cm (12 inches) on the other to allow space for hot pots and ingredients during cooking.

38 cm
(15 inches)

30 cm
(12 inches)

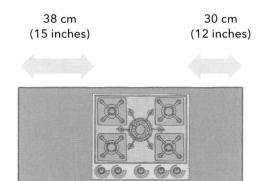

SINKS

Sinks come in many arrangements: single, double, and triple, with single- or double-drainers. To some extent the need for deep sinks or multiple sinks is affected by the ownership of a dishwasher, and again the complexity of what you do in the kitchen. But it is worth remembering that deep sinks are not always needed or easy to use, and filling them uses a great deal of water. If you choose a two-sink arrangement, it is often worth having a mix of sizes so that one is used for large items or for washing up and the other for rinsing. The small sink on some double sinks that is set next to a large sink, is usually used to feed into a waste disposal unit, but it can still be useful even if you don't have such a device.

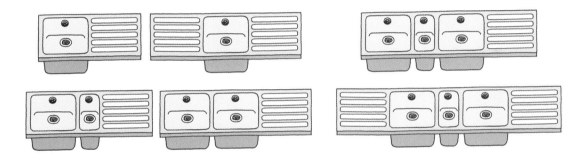

SINK MATERIALS

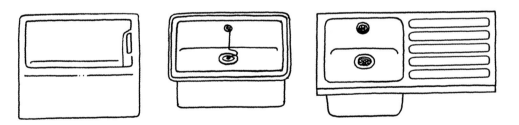

The choice of material for sinks includes stainless steel, porcelain, enamelled steel, composite, and resin. If you have composite work surfaces fitted, it is common to have a built-in sink constructed with the same material and finished to become part of a continuous surface. These are extremely hardy and easy to clean but very expensive. Stainless steel sinks are probably the most common and are fairly affordable. They are also very tough and easily cleaned. Porcelain sinks (such as 'butler sinks') are as tough but often very deep and impractical for washing up on a daily basis without the use of a separate bowl. They can be marked by heavy metal objects and if actually scratched are difficult to repair. Enamelled metal sinks are also possible to mark or damage but will have a reasonable life if treated well.

TAPS

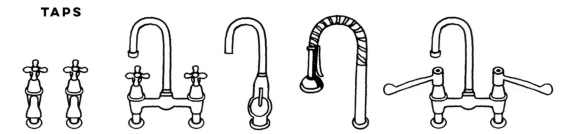

While the use of taps goes back perhaps thousands of years in their simplest form, the modern tap is probably only several hundred years old, and the mixer tap just over 100 years old. While separate taps are perfectly usable, a mixer tap is extremely convenient in the kitchen. There are variations of the mixer tap that have progressed from the twin tap to a mixer lever that controls temperature and flow. These lever taps are much easier to use (in my opinion…). It is also increasingly common to have a spray tap for washing items in the sink. These have been common in commercial restaurants for many years but more home-friendly versions are available. Another type of tap that is worth considering are those with particularly long levers. These are similar in style to those used in hospitals to avoid contamination, and they avoid spreading dirt and are easy for all members of the family to operate.

U-BENDS & WASTE DISPOSAL

Most sinks have a U-bend below the outlet. This acts as a trap for anything small dropped down the plughole but its main purpose is to stop smells from returning up the drainage system. These U-bends can occasionally block but are fairly easily to unblock. The first thing to try is a plunger if you have one, but be aware that it may not work unless you cover the overflow with something like a wet cloth so it will allow pressure to build up as you plunge. You can try using very hot water as often the pipe will block if fat hardens in it after someone has tipped it away (not recommended). Failing that you can try a chemical sink un-blocker, but you can also place a bucket below the U-bend and release the cap on the underside of the bend. This can be smelly and unpleasant so gloves are a good idea.

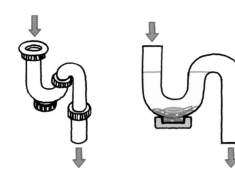

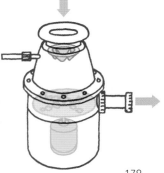

Waste disposal units are also fixed below sink outlets. They work by having a motor drive a grinding disk to break up waste into particles small enough to wash down the drain.

KITCHEN LAYOUT

There are a number of factors to take into consideration when planning the layout of a kitchen, including: the shape of the space; budget; the number of cooks working at the same time; complexity and style of cooking; safety; number of eaters; and function as a social space as well as a cooking space. There are three main basic kitchen shapes.

GALLEY KITCHEN

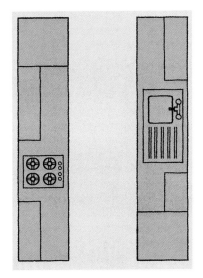 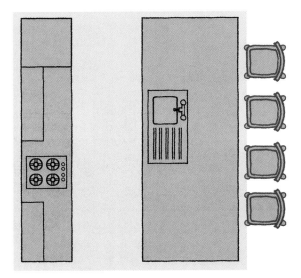

The narrow kitchens with working areas on both sides of a central walkway are referred to as galley kitchens and are very common. In commercial kitchens the actual workspace any chef will have often conforms to this layout, as space is often restricted and the shape can be very efficient. It is not good if the space has to double as a walkway for others to pass through. The arrangement of the units, hob, and sink, etc., should, if possible, hold with the triangle for placement. It is not a great social space for entertaining unless you have an open side to the kitchen, in which case one of the work surfaces can double up as a breakfast bar, as shown above.

L-SHAPED KITCHEN

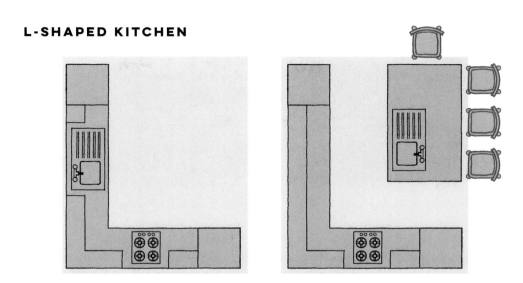

The 'L-shaped' kitchen is a sensible approach for anyone that doesn't have to fit into a narrow space, and using two walls set at a 90° angle makes it very ergonomic if laid out well. The L can be enhanced by placing a table or island unit that adds a working area and also a place to eat.

U-SHAPED KITCHEN

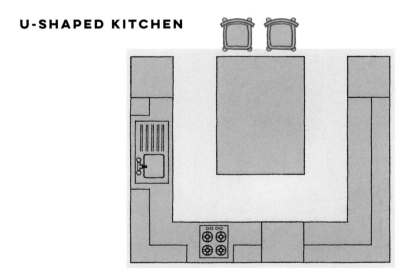

The U-shaped kitchen allows for both a large number of units and for two or more people to work together easily in the space. When laying out a larger kitchen in a U-shape, consider how the tasks are divided and design zones for those tasks in a logical sequence around the space to reduce having to keep moving backward and forwards around the kitchen.

KITCHEN LAYOUT TIPS

Of course, the space will define a lot of the layout of a kitchen, but the process of preparing food has an order to it, and if the kitchen is designed to move the food along though the kitchen from raw until it is finally served, this can make life a lot easier.

Store crockery and glasses near the sink/dishwasher.

Do not store food in cupboards that are affected by heat from hobs and ovens.

Bear in mind that water should be separated from electric outlets.

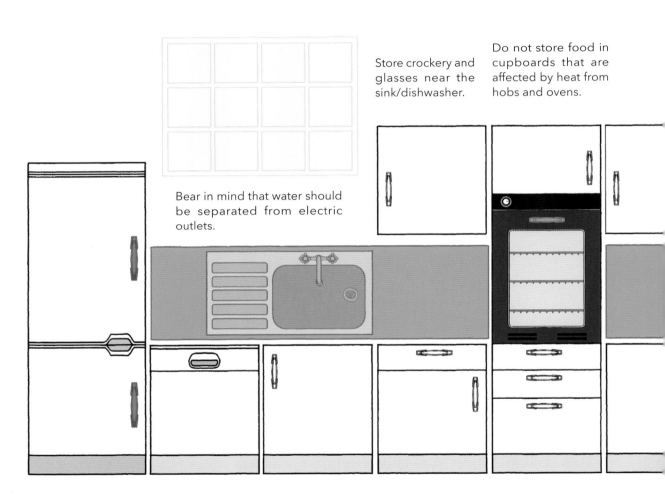

Fridges are useful near the sink as many food items will need washing.

Placing a dishwasher by the sink will allow you to sort items for hand or machine washing and also allow the drainage and water supply to work for both.

Placing a drawer for cutlery by the sink is really convenient as it can be close to both the sink and the dishwasher.

Herbs, spices, and cooking oils should be kept near the hob and oven.

Windows should be located at a distance from gas hobs so that an open window will not blow out a flame, or affect cooking.

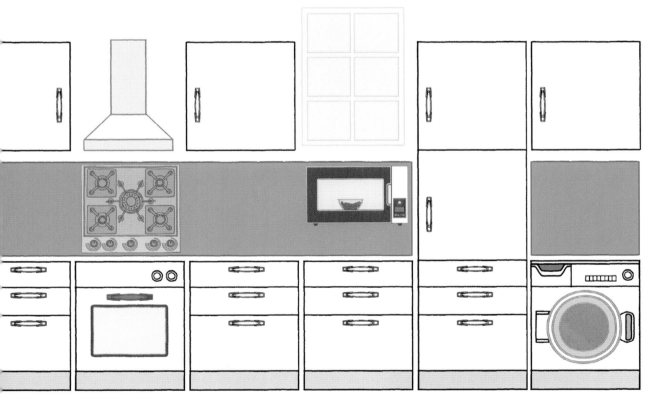

Store pots and pans close to the stove.

Bakery ingredients, mixing bowls, and tins should be kept close to the oven.

Washing machines and sinks are often placed on an outside wall so that they have access to drainage. Organizing plumbing in other ways is possible but can vastly increase costs.

HYGIENE & SAFETY

Food hygiene is important! In a kitchen, you are managing a situation where not only you but bacteria exist, and if given the opportunity, bacteria can and will multiply, causing potentially serious problems. If there was an order of things that are important about food, the first and foremost would be that food has to be health-giving and nourishing. And to this end you should care and respect the kitchen, the food, and those you are feeding. This stems from hygienic background environments and processes, and well-kept equipment and ingredients.

CLEANLINESS & DRESS

The single most common cause of food contamination is via dirty hands. This can be very largely reduced by washing, but most people do not follow the recommended practice for washing their hands. While this may seem extreme, it is a small price to pay for a reduction in irritating and potentially dangerous infections.

HAND WASHING

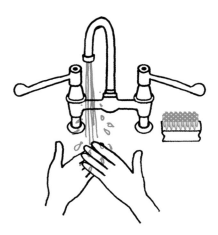

[1] Thoroughly wet both your hand and nail brush. If you have lever taps, use your elbow to turn them.

[2] Add soap to your hands.

[3] Work the soap in the palms of your hands thoroughly.

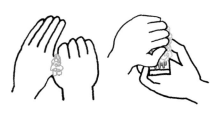

[4] Rub the lather well around your fingers, including their bases.

[5] Work soap over thumbs and scrub fingertips and nails.

[6] Dry with a clean cloth and turn off the tap without touching it with your washed hands.

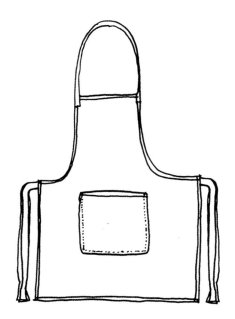

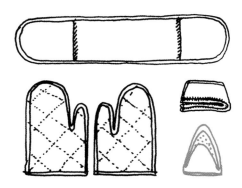

WHAT TO WEAR?

An apron is a very good option for the kitchen as it not only keeps your clothes clean but also is easily washed and ready as a hygienic garment when you need it.

OVEN GLOVES

Oven gloves are safe if of a decent quality. The major problem is if they become damp, because they can then transmit heat. This can be resolved by using silicone gloves or pot holders.

FIRES IN THE KITCHEN

In has been stated that 47% of fires in the home are not reported to the fire service. The fire service recommend that you never take risks if you have a fire, and that you should get anybody in the house out and close all doors. But they also say that you shouldn't tackle a fire unless you are confident that you can manage it, have the right equipment to do so, and don't attempt to do so if the fire is starting to spread beyond its starting place.

The general advice is that if you wish to have some safety equipment, then go for a fire blanket and/or a water mist type extinguisher. Both of these may help in the fighting of fat fires as well as more general fires. Do not under any circumstance try to fight a fat fire with water, but if safe to do so turn off the heat (not leaning over the fire), and smother it with either device if it can be safely done. If purchasing a fire blanket make sure that they are fit for purpose and that they cover the types of fire that happen within a kitchen. Most firefighting devices are printed with codes that define what they are safe to use for.

CLEANING

Certain items in the kitchen are damaged by the wrong cleaning method so some basic rules should be followed.

CHOPPING BOARDS

Plastic chopping boards should be washed with washing-up liquid and water, then soak in a mix of water and bleach (1 teaspooon per 2 litres of water) for 10 minutes; allow to dry on a draining board.

Scrub with water and detergent, and allow to air-dry. When a deeper clean is required you can use a paste of water and baking soda and then rinse with hot water.

STAINLESS STEEL

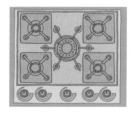

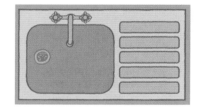

Stainless steel hobs and sinks are prone to a build up of tiny scratches that dull the surface. These are best removed with a cream cleaner designed for the purpose. These creams are abrasive as well but use very fine particles to create finer scratches (which in fact is what happens in most polishing processes).

OVENS

Some modern ovens now have self-cleaning modes that are in fact a very high baking cycle. What dirt is in the oven will turn to ash and once the oven is cooled you can wipe it clean. Ovens without this function often have an enamel interior surface that is resistant to heavy duty chemical cleaners, but when using these cleaners, be very careful to avoid getting them on seals around the door or any other part of the oven or yourself. Gloves should be worn.

FRIDGES & FREEZERS

Aim for a time when you have reduced the amount of food in it to a minimum as the process will thaw any food and make it unsafe to freeze. Once emptied and defrosted, remove all drawers and shelves and wash in soapy water. If you have cold glass shelves, let them warm up before plunging them in hot water to avoid breaking. The interior can then be washed with a strong solution of baking powder in water.

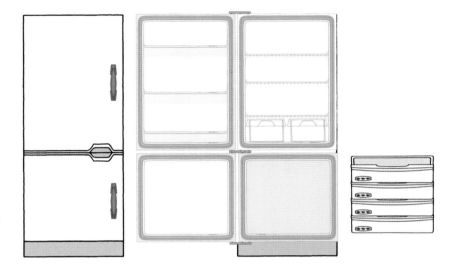

WORKTOPS

Oiled wooden worktops should be wiped with a detergent/water mix, then dried, and then if necessary wiped with oil.

Laminated surfaces vary in quality so be careful if trying to remove stains with anything tougher than a sponge and a cream cleaner.

Composite surfaces are very safe to clean as they are chemically stable and as a solid there is no danger of breaking through the surface.

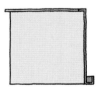

Stainless steel is best wiped down, and hardened dirt soaked and removed with a blunt wooden implement.

For marble, use a spray of soapy water and then wipe dry with a cloth. Avoid anything acid (like lemon juice or vinegar).

For granite, use an antibacterial granite cleaner daily or mild soapy solution. If it has been sealed, check with the manufacturer first.

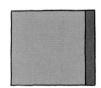

Slate should be wiped with a soft cloth and mild solution of detergent and, again, avoiding acids.

WASHING UP

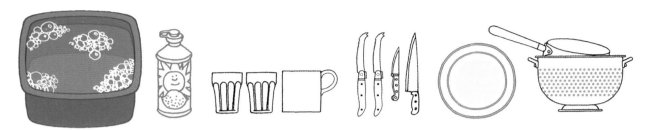

Washing up by hand is greatly aided by wearing gloves – using them means you can increase the temperature of the water, which not only helps with grease break-down, but can also help destroy bacteria. It may also seem obvious but it is worth scraping away any food you can before the actual wash. Wash items in order – glasses and drinking containers, then cutlery, then other crockery, then pans, etc. Use a wire stacker and allow things to air-dry if possible, but if you want to put things away, then make sure they are very dry as even damp plates can promote the growth of bacteria.

BRUSHES, CLOTHS & SCOURERS

While very useful, washing-up cloths, brushes, and scourers often harbour bacteria. To avoid this regularly machine-wash the cloths and put the brushes in a dishwasher. For non-metal scourers and sponges, dampen them and place in a microwave oven for 40 seconds.

BE CAREFUL

Wiping and scrubbing can damage the surface of most materials but using a softer material than the surface to be cleaned will inflict less damage. So avoid hard scourers on soft materials such as using a steel scourer on a copper pan, or a scouring pad on almost any plastic.

DISHWASHING MACHINES

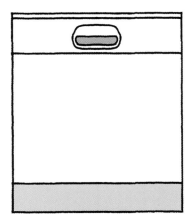

It is pretty much as energy-efficient to use a dishwashing machine as doing a hand-wash if the machine is full or used on an economy cycle. It is often more hygienic in a dishwasher too. As with hand-washing, it is advisable to scrape the plates, etc., well before loading them into the machine.

The salt that is added to the machine is responsible for the shine and avoidance of limescale build-up in the machine. It works by removing the calcium and magnesium ions present in hard water. Unlike table salt, it does not contain anti-caking agents and will not clog the dishwasher's softener unit.

Also… do not try using hand-washing up liquid in a dishwashing machine as dishwashing detergent is somewhat different and doesn't foam like hand-washing liquid. I learnt this to my own cost and filled half the kitchen with foam in the process…

DON'T DISHWASH!

FOOD HYGIENE

Food is part of the natural cycle of things that grow and then degrade. We gather food that is alive and it starts to break down almost immediately. For some foods this is part of what we want, and we go out of our way to control that 'break down' (as with yogurt, cheese, beer, wine, etc.). Bacteria and fungi such as yeasts, play a vital part in this process, but not always to our advantage. When we want to preserve food for our own consumption but want to extend the time before it becomes unpalatable or even dangerous, the usual method is to slow or halt the growth of bacteria or fungi. This is done by controlling the environment in and around the food, with either heat or chemical controls. Too high or low a temperature or too acid or alkali an environment (as with pickling) can slow, stop, or kill bacteria or fungi. Different bacteria and fungi are resistant to different extents, so treatment of food has to cover many bases.

Bacteria and fungal spores are in almost every environment. Most foods carry them (at least on their surface). Some are much more dangerous than others to humans, with some only dangerous in certain circumstances. So over time and the application of science, rules have developed as to how to safely handle, prepare, cook, serve, and store food.

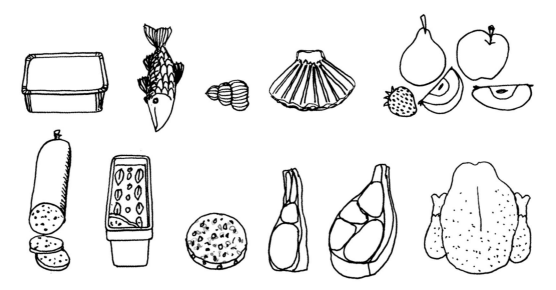

The fact that bacteria will sit on the outside of meat means that it is important not to break the surface and allow bacteria to enter. It is good practice during the slaughter and processing of meat that this is carefully observed. In the home, when preparing anything from cut or minced (ground) meat, you should be aware that bacteria will likely have been mixed into it and that it may well be best to cook it immediately. This is why any pâté or terrine that is made from chopped or minced (ground) meat should be cooked until it is safe.

FOOD & SAFE TEMPERATURES

The question of what constitutes a safe temperature is a complex one. Bacteria will grow faster in warm temperatures, but will die or become spores at higher temperatures. At fridge temperatures (0–5°C/32–41°F), their growth will slow, and when frozen at -20°C (-4°F) (the temperatures most freezers operate at), they will remain inert and will not breed. Generally speaking, a danger zone exists between the temperatures of 5°C and 50°C (41 and 122°F). Keeping food between these temperatures may well be very risky, particularly for certain foods:

- Meats including beef, pork, chicken, fish, and other seafood
- Eggs and unfermented dairy products (cheese is an exception but unpasteurized cheese should be avoided by children, those with a low immune system, and pregnant women)
- Prepared fresh fruit and vegetables
- Cooked dishes that include meat, vegetables, beans, rice, pasta, etc.
- Sauces, such as gravy
- Raw and cooked sprouts

These items should be stored in a fridge (if cooked they should be allowed to cool before placing them in the fridge).

When heated above 50°C (122°F), bacteria start to die. And as the heat increases, more and more will die. At boiling point, many bacteria perish but not all. This is when pressure cooking can be used to raise the temperature further and kill spores. A standard pressure cooker will raise the temperature to 115°C (239°F), which will kill almost everything …but not all.

PASCALIZATION

Pascalization is the process of killing bacteria by using pressure. While pressure cookers do apply pressure, this on its own is not enough to kill many bacteria, so special machinery is used to generate extreme pressure. This is often done when a food's flavour is badly affected by heat. Currently it is becoming more common and is seen listed on some fruit juices, where pascalization kills the bacteria, and the spores they leave behind are unable to survive in the acid environment of a fruit juice.

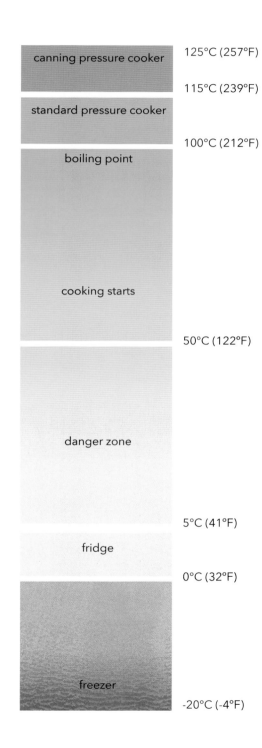

canning pressure cooker	125°C (257°F)
	115°C (239°F)
standard pressure cooker	
boiling point	100°C (212°F)
cooking starts	
	50°C (122°F)
danger zone	
	5°C (41°F)
fridge	
	0°C (32°F)
freezer	
	-20°C (-4°F)

USING A FRIDGE SAFELY

There are certain practices in the use of fridges that can avoid problems with contamination and spoiling. These include:

 1 Never place hot food in the fridge. By doing so you may raise the temperature of the other food and create a dangerous situation. Instead, cool the food, firstly by taking it off /out of the cooker, and allowing it to cool while covered. When the pot is just hand-warm, it is worth cooling it rapidly by using running water or placing the pan/container in a bowl of iced water. This will take the temperature down rapidly through the 'danger zone'. Make sure cooked food is placed in the fridge within 2 hours, and then consumed within 3 days.

 2 Do not leave the door open beyond the time necessary to place or retrieve items. This will reduce the running cost of the fridge and also help to keep the temperature constant and safe. The safe temperature zone is 0–5°C (32–41°F).

 3 Food and drink should be stacked in the fridge to reduce any chance of cross contamination. Raw foods should be placed below ready-to-eat and cooked foods so that any dripping will not cause contamination. Raw meats and fish should be kept separately and in sealed containers on the bottom shelf (the coldest part) of the fridge.

 4 Fruit and vegetables kept in the fridge should be kept in sealed bags or containers and should be washed before use as they can still carry and grow certain bacteria at low temperatures.

FOODS THAT ARE BETTER NOT KEPT IN THE FRIDGE

Certain foods are better not kept in the fridge for a number of different reasons. Bread and cakes when baked convert starch to more complex chemicals, but placing them in a cold environment will cause the starch to reconvert to a basic starch. This affects the texture and creates a stale taste. Temporarily this starch can be softened by heating but it will harden again as it cools.

Cheese is better kept cool but not as cold as a fridge. The flavour will greatly benefit by not being chilled.

Tomatoes also suffer when chilled as the chemicals that give the more complex flavours are destroyed by chilling.

FREEZERS

The home freezer became popular in the second half of the 20th century. In earlier times some people kept ice boxes to preserve food and would have deliveries of fresh ice to put in them, but the cooling effect of ice was adequate for refrigeration but not the freezing of food. Freezing has many advantages over other forms of storage in that it hardly affects flavour and the 'shelf-life' is greatly extended. If the food is very rapidly frozen, the crystals of water within the food that form as the water becomes ice are very small. This has a very limited effect on the structure of the food so when the food is defrosted it has a better structure/texture. Slow freezing can cause very large crystals to form and this can greatly damage the food's texture. So, it's better if possible to reduce the size of foods you want to freeze so they can freeze more quickly (as residual heat in a large object will slow the cooling of the whole mass).

As with fridges, never put warm or hot food in a freezer. Allow it to cool first and then place it in a suitable container or bag. These should be waterproof and be able to withstand the cold without becoming brittle (quite a lot of plastics are actually unsuitable for this reason). Mark the container with the date of freezing and if there is any chance that it will look similar to any other dish when frozen, then mark what it is as well. Try to make sure that food is in a thin single layer so it can freeze quickly, and do not stack unfrozen food containers together, but make sure that they have space between them to aid freezing.

Freezers store food at approximately -20°C (-4°F). While this freezes pure water, if the food is very high in sugars or alcohol, then it still may not freeze. Over time, this will allow large crystals to form and the food to degrade. High-sugar foods in particular (such as ice creams and frozen desserts) may change texture very quickly so it isn't a good idea to keep them for long periods.

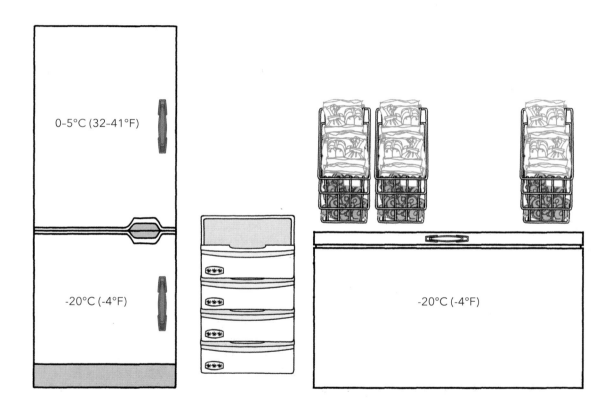

In a large freezer it is worth considering a system so you can work through foods before they have reached their useful storage life. Use wire baskets if provided, as this can greatly ease moving food around to reach whatever you are looking for, and they can be used as a filing system for bagged food for easy access. Keeping similar foods together can also work as a system: fruits, vegetables, meat, cooked meals, sauces, etc.

HIGH-RISK FOODS

The risk attached to most foods is generally very low, but certain foods do have potential for much higher levels of risk. There are some people that are more susceptible to these foods and some foods have particular dangers for some people.

The risks can be broadly divided into four categories:

- microbial and viral
- chemical toxicity
- parisites
- allergenic

There are some foods that, due to their very nature, carry these risks at a higher level than other foods, but with care the risks can be reduced.

BACTERIAL RISKS

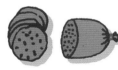

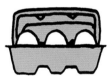

Bean sprouts grow in almost the perfect warm, damp environment for a number of unpleasant bacteria to thrive in. They can cause food poisoning and it is far safer to eat them cooked.

Cold cooked meats, **cured meats**, and **pâtés** are often eaten without cooking so if carrying any risks these will not be destroyed. Unless you are very sure about their safety, avoid feeding them to pregnant women or anybody from a vulnerable group.

Eggs pose some threat from salmonella in the yolk, white, and on the shell, but the risk is reduced if you avoid cracked or broken shells. Store eggs below 5°C (41°F) in the fridge, and if you do use them raw do not feed to children or pregnant women.

Fish starts to break down as soon as it is dead and therefore can become a risk very quickly from developing bacteria. It can also carry parasites. These can be killed by deep freezing (far below home freezing temperatures), and this process is used for 'sushi-grade' fish that is eaten raw. All fish should be kept correctly stored as if it is not it can develop histamine, which can be toxic and is not destroyed by normal cooking. As a rule be very careful with fish, and make sure it is cooked adequately, and that it is kept separate from other foods.

Fruit can carry listeria so should be thoroughly washed before eating. Some **berries**, **chillies**, **tomatoes**, and **peppers** can carry salmonella, so again should be handled with care and washed extremely well if you must use them raw.

Poultry is high-risk as it can carry campylobacter and salmonella and therefore should be handled carefully. Don't wash raw chicken as this can spread any bacteria. Clean all surfaces, implements, and containers that poultry comes into contact with.

Raw greens that are eaten in salads, etc., can carry E. coli or contamination from animals or chemicals. Always wash them thoroughly.

Raw milk is unpasteurized and can carry a number of bacteria that can give you food poisoning, as well as tuberculosis (although this is now very rare).

Rice carries bacteria that are activated when the rice is cooked. These will develop if the rice is stored badly once cooked so you should keep cooked rice only for short periods and under 5°C (41°F).

Shellfish are vulnerable to carrying algae that carry toxins. They also can carry high levels of mercury that they collect as they feed. When shellfish die, they break down very quickly and should be avoided. So always make sure they are alive prior to eating/cooking.

Soft cheeses should be avoided by pregnant women and vulnerable people as the cheese can carry staphylococcus.

TOXIC RISKS

There are some foods that do pose a toxic risk, including raw beans (especially kidney beans), cassava, and nutmeg.

Raw beans such as kidney beans carry a protein called haemagglutinin, which is poisonous. It can be reduced by soaking and actually destroyed by rapid boiling. If you are going to use uncooked beans in a recipe, soak overnight, bring them to the boil for a few minutes, and then reduce the heat to let them cook through (or alternatively, use cooked canned beans).

Cassava is eaten in many parts of the world and in its raw, unpeeled state it is toxic. It can be bought canned and ready to cook with, but if you wish to cook it from raw please seek advice.

Nutmeg can also be toxic but in large quantities is so strong-tasting and unpleasant that it takes determination to poison yourself.

PARASITES

Parasites do occur in some common foods (including **meat** and **fish**), but also from contamination by animals. Almost all of them can be killed by thorough cooking or deep freezing (-40°C/-40°F and below for a period of days). This is how **sushi** and **sashimi** is prepared to make it safe.

General advice is to maintain good hygiene in the kitchen, cook meat and fish well (with particular care if serving to a vulnerable person), and wash **leafy vegetables** very well.

DRYING FOOD

Preserving food is about creating conditions where any degradation is slowed or stopped. Bacteria is affected by a number of things, including moisture level. By removing the moisture you slow or stop its activity and/or ability to grow. Salt levels in food can often actually kill bacteria, and this is done by drawing out water from the bacteria's cells. A wide range of food was dried in the past before the invention of canning and refrigeration, and techniques were developed that created unique foods that are now part of our cuisine. Drying often intensifies flavour or helps to develop new tastes and aromas.

The simplest methods are air- and sun-drying, but if the food contains sugars that are hydroscopic (i.e. they cling on to water), additional heat may have to be applied to reduce the moisture level. Once dried, foods can have a very long shelf life if kept away from moisture. Therefore it is sensible to keep dried foods in a container that shields them from moisture in the outside environment. Foods which are less hydroscopic are easier to preserve but even these may degrade through evaporation or flavour loss. Herbs are prone to this and it is worth checking dried herbs for loss of quality and replace them if necessary.

Note that home drying can be carried out on some foods by simply putting the food in a dry, warm place and waiting. This will work for herbs but not for many other foods as it isn't quick enough to prevent bacteria from degrading the food. Sun-drying can work but the background atmospheric humidity must be lower than 20% and this is not common.

PREPARING FRUIT FOR HOME-DRYING

[1] Select very fresh produce, and discard any damaged fruit.

[2] Remove stems, stones, and seeds and cut the food into thin slices – this reduces drying time greatly.

[3] Some fruits will be liable to browning in air. This effect can be reduced by soaking in a dilution of ascorbic acid (vitamin C), or sodium bisulfite. Sodium bisulfite can cause allergic reactions, though.

[4] To reduce spoilage, increase shelf life, and soften skins (that may become tough with drying), you can blanch fruit (or vegetables) in boiling water, or in a steamer, then cool them in iced water, dry, and place in the dehydrator, oven, or dryer (see right).

OVEN-DRYING

Oven-drying does work. The prepared food is placed on trays in the oven on a low heat and the oven door is left open. This takes two or three times longer than a dehydrator/food dryer unless the oven has an effective fan. Food dehydrators/dryers are the best option if you wish to dry food regularly.

HOME DRYERS/ DEHYDRATORS

Food dehydrators/dryers create a moving flow of warmed air that passes up through racks of prepared food. This warms the food slightly, encouraging evaporation, and serves a secondary purpose in that it carries off the damp vapour.

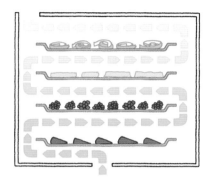

Purchased home dryers are usually very simple and have racks for the food, a heater, and a fan. They may vary in design but the capacity is the main factor that you should consider once you decide on a reliable brand. It is also possible to purchase or build an outdoor dryer that uses the sun's heat to dry the food. It works by heating a darkened panel, which in turn heats air, which rises due to convection through a chamber where the food is exposed to it.

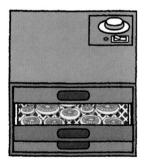

USING A MICROWAVE TO DRY HERBS

You can use a microwave oven to dry herbs and some leafy vegetables. Place a few small sprigs of them on paper towels in the microwave and heat for 2–3 minutes, then check to see if they are brittle. If not run for another 30 seconds and check again.

BIBLIOGRAPHY

Listed here are books, websites and sources that I have some direct knowledge of and have respect for. Some may seem a little uncommon, but will, I hope, aid those who are curious about the culinary world.

BOOKS ABOUT FOOD FOR THOSE THAT JUST LOVE FOOD

The Pleasures of the Table by Jean Anthelme Brillat-Savarin
An amusing classic, and well worth a read, by a man who loved his food and thought about it a lot. First published in 1825, but still relevant, and the source of some of the greatest quotations about food.

Ma Gastronomie by Fernand Point
While it's improbable that one could ever aspire to cook to the level of Fernand Point's restaurant, the book is far more than recipes. It celebrates a life of generous cooking and the joy of eating.

BOOKS FOR THOSE INTRIGUED BY PROFESSIONAL COOKS

The Kitchen Book/The Cook Book by Nicolas Freeling
Two books of cooking now bound as one. Before becoming a writer of crime fiction Nicolas Freeling was a chef. In these two books he covers his early years in France, the misery of post-war British food and very good general advice on cooking.

Kitchen Confidential: Adventures in the culinary underbelly by Anthony Bourdain
The book that made Anthony Bourdain the idol of every tattooed chef by spilling the beans on the raw life behind the professional kitchen doors. Sex, drugs and rock 'n' roll (and cooking).

Blood, Bones and Butter: The inadvertent education of a reluctant chef by Gabrielle Hamilton
A very well written autobiography of a woman who ended up a great chef. I found it interesting, touching and informative. The book covers her life from childhood to setting up her own restaurant via an interesting and very human journey through life. Childhood memories of cooking whole lamb for parties lead to tales of fighting with neighbours while trying to run a decent restaurant.

The Sweet Life in Paris: Delicious adventures in the world's most glorious and perplexing city by David Lebovitz
An interesting, funny and insightful book about Paris, the French and food by an American pastry chef and food blogger.

REFERENCE BOOKS ON FOOD AND COOKERY

McGee on Food and Cooking: An encyclopedia of kitchen science, history and culture by Harold McGee
This is simply the best source for understanding the kitchen. A masterpiece!

The Oxford Companion to Food by Alan Davidson
A huge and very informative guide to all things food – it covers more food culture that McGee but with a little less science. A great work.

Modernist Cuisine: The art and science of cooking (6 volume set) by Nathan Myhrvold
Huge volumes covering the science of cookery, with original research, amazing photography and excellent writing. These are expensive to buy, but if considered as part of an education they are a worthwhile purchase for the professional cook.

BOOKS ABOUT ACTUAL COOKING TO LEARN FROM

While there are many books that cover a vast array or the world's cuisine one has to start somewhere…

Delia's Complete Cookery Course (Classic Edition: Volumes 1–3) by Delia Smith
Almost bulletproof recipes that produce decent results. If you're looking for place to start, these books are probably it.

Then if you want to step it up a notch…

The Food Lab: Better home cooking through science by J. Kenji López-alt
A scientific approach to cookery, laid out clearly and well, by a man who does his own research and testing. If you were to work your way through this book it would give a solid base to your cookery.

Mastering the Art of French Cooking (Volume 1) by Julia Child with Louisette Bertholle and Simone Beck
This book by America's great educator on food, really does work. She researched and tested everything after spending time training and eating in France.

And for a little more understanding…

Cooking for Geeks: Real science, great cooks and good food by Jeff Potter
'As it says on the tin.' Using a simple approach it covers many of the techniques in vogue with 'modernist' cookery, but in a do-able way, and with clear explanation.

And for cocktails and understanding of flavour…

Liquid Intelligence: The art and science of the perfect cocktail by Dave Arnold
This is an astonishing book that goes deep into the art and science of cocktails. Quite equipment and science heavy, but a bible for hardcore geeky bartenders.

Drinks: Unravelling the mysteries of flavour and aroma in drink by Tony Conigliaro
This is quite a technical book by the man behind top cocktail bars and consultant to restaurateurs and others seeking top-notch help with flavour development.

For baking…

Momofuku Milk Bar by Christina Tosi
An amazing bakery (if slightly left-field) by the extraordinary people behind the cakes and desserts for Momofuku. It is worth searching 'Christina Tosi' online and watching her baking tutorials.

For ice cream…

The Perfect Scoop: Ice creams, sorbets, granitas, and sweet accessories by David Lebovitz
Top-notch recipes that really work.

Ice Creams, Sorbets and Gelati: The definitive guide by Caroline and Robin Weir
A huge, informative book that covers history and science as well as providing great recipes. Gives enough information to help you to develop your own recipes that work.

INDEX